PORTFOLIO PENGUIN

# MRS MONEYPENNY'S FINANCIAL ADVICE FOR INDEPENDENT WOMEN

'If financial ineptitude is holding you back in your relationships, or your professional life, then this book should be the cure. It makes it simple to be really smart about money' Anne Ashworth, *The Times*

'Mrs Moneypenny has provided women of our time with a comprehensive and easily digestible guide on how to become financially independent' Helena Morrisey, CEO, Newton Investment Management and Founder, 30% Club

'Mrs Moneypenny walks us through the perils and pitfalls of personal finance, offering tips and examples from her own life – and makes a persuasive case for the need for gender-specific advice for independent women everywhere' Justine Roberts, CEO, Mumsnet

'Ignore your personal finances and you ignore the means to fulfil your own potential as a woman. Don't do that – read this book instead' Sarah Brown, President, Theirworld

'Mrs Moneypenny is back with her unique brand of no-nonsense, practical, confidence-building guidance. Any woman who thinks of herself as financially challenged can relax. Step by step, *Mrs Moneypenny's Financial Advice for Independent Women* will spur you to get on top of your money before it gets on top of you' Ashley Milne-Tyte, host of The Broad Experience podcast on women and the workplace

'By investing in this book you are taking the first steps towards managing your financial independence' Nancy Dell'Olio

'Whatever you earn or owe, Mrs Moneypenny can help' Jeannette Winterson, author of *Why Be Happy When You Could Be Normal?*

'This wise and empathetic book shows every woman, however small her earnings, how to gain financial independence. It is full of practical tips for everyone who might need the financial back-up to leave her boss or her boyfriend!' Eve Pollard, former editor of the *Sunday Mirror* and the *Sunday Express*

‘Don’t be fooled by the title – a great deal of Mrs Moneypenny’s financial advice for women is equally useful for men. It’s also exactly the kind of book we should be giving to young people as they begin to navigate the daunting world of finance’ Dr Anthony Seldon, author of *Blair Unbound* and *New Labour, Old Labour*

‘A great read packed full of practical must dos that will inspire you to take control of the finances in your life. Whilst aimed at women, it’s a useful financial life guide for everybody. The homework at the end of every chapter eliminates any excuses; you will feel motivated to take control and feel better about your financial life’ Steven Cooper, Head of Personal and Business Banking, UK, Barclays

‘Her style is incisive, self-deprecating and hilarious. Her advice is frank, tough and businesslike. She is funny and wise, and her wisdom comes from taking her career seriously but never herself’ Cilla Snowball, Group Chairman and CEO, Abbott Mead Vickers BBDO

‘I wish I had ended up as worldly wise, energetic and well-connected as she plainly is’ Bill Emmott, former editor, the *Economist*

‘Who needs Bond when Mrs Moneypenny comes to our rescue every Saturday?’ Stephen Hester, CEO, RSA

‘Mrs M. is the *FT*’s sexy little secret . . . she writes with great wit and deftness’ David Yelland, former Editor, the *Sun*

## ABOUT THE AUTHORS

For fifteen years **Mrs Moneypenny** has been entertaining readers of the *Financial Times* with her weekly column. She presented the Channel 4 series *Superscrimpers*, and the Mrs Moneypenny show has run at the Edinburgh Fringe, off-Broadway and the Hay Festival. She is the best-selling author of *Mrs Moneypenny’s Careers Advice for Ambitious Women* and *Mrs Moneypenny: Survival in the City* (ebook only).

**Heather McGregor** owns and runs Taylor Bennett, the executive search firm. She is a committed philanthropist in the area of employability and social mobility, having founded the Taylor Bennett Foundation in 2008, and is currently chair of Career Academies Foundation. In 2014 she was named as one of *GQ*’s 100 Most Connected Women.

www.MrsMoneyPenny.com

# MRS MONEYPENNY'S FINANCIAL ADVICE FOR INDEPENDENT WOMEN

Mrs Moneypenny
with Heather McGregor

PORTFOLIO
PENGUIN

PORTFOLIO PENGUIN

UK | USA | Canada | Ireland | Australia
India | New Zealand | South Africa

Penguin Books is part of the Penguin Random House group of companies
whose addresses can be found at global.penguinrandomhouse.com.

First published by Portfolio Penguin 2014
This edition published 2015
001



Every effort has been made to ensure that the information contained in this book is complete and accurate. However, neither the publisher nor the author is engaged in rendering financial, legal or other professional services to the individual reader. If you require financial, legal or other expert assistance, you should seek the services of a competent professional.



Typeset by Jouve (UK), Milton Keynes
Printed in Great Britain by Clays Ltd, St Ives plc

A CIP catalogue record for this book is available from the British Library

ISBN: 978-0-670-92330-4

www.greenpenguin.co.uk

Penguin Random House is committed to a sustainable future for our business, our readers and our planet. This book is made from Forest Stewardship Council® certified paper.

This book is dedicated to My Cleverest Girlfriend, Merryn Somerset Webb, who gave up a lucrative career in stockbroking to launch *MoneyWeek*. She was part of the original development of *SuperScrimpers*, and co-presented the first series with me. Merryn has inspired me, and thousands of others, to take their finances in hand. Her writing has blazed a trail for everyone who wants to make money funny and interesting and sexy.

'Anyone can understand finance; it's not difficult.'

RENÉE ELLIOTT,
*entrepreneur and founder of Planet Organic*

# CONTENTS

# INTRODUCTION

Who is this book for? This book is for every woman who wants to be financially independent, and by that, I mean independent of her parents, her partner and even the state. All three of these can play a part in financial support along life's journey – there are times, indeed, when they should – but hopefully not for ever.

In short, the purpose of this book is to get you to think about your finances more, and ultimately to take control of them.

This book is *not* designed to be a wholly comprehensive directory of financial products; that is a function far better performed by an advisory website, given just how often regulations change and new products appear. This is designed to be a book that will make you think about every area of your financial life, and challenge yourself to take steps towards reaching your own financial finish line: the defined amount of money you need to earn in your lifetime.

Women need more financial knowledge than men. We live longer and need to provide for ourselves for longer while, statistically, we earn less money than men over an average lifetime. It is often the inevitable result of taking time out to have children but, of course, women who do not have children may have career breaks forced on them too. Elderly parents, a partner who is posted abroad, or illness can all mean that there may be times when a full-time focus on your career is not possible or desirable.

But perhaps the main reason why I believe the time is right for a call to women to take charge of their own finances is because I think there is a more fundamental reason that explains why they are holding back from doing so, and that is a lack of confidence. Women suffer more from this than men, and in the area of finance – so set about by jargon and idiosyncrasies – it's all too easy to become intimidated.

What I have learned, and want to share with the readers of this book, is that sorting out your finances – whether you want to make better investments, reduce your debt, buy a house or just get better educated financially – takes time. I saw this so often when I was making *SuperScrimpers*, the TV show that I presented for three years on Channel 4. Almost everyone that I came across during filming, from the people I spoke to on the programme, to the crew and the make-up artists, were able to improve their finances by investing more time.

Even I needed to invest more time, I realized.

During the latter part of the Olympics, in August 2012, I took myself off to a clinic in Austria to invest some time in my physical health. I had never done anything like this before, and it was a revelation. My first few days were spent surviving on a daily ration of about

350 calories. I was issued with two tiny pieces of toast for breakfast and instructed to eat them in small portions, each of which I was to chew forty times. I was so exhausted after tackling the first piece of toast that I abandoned the other and went to lie down. Lunch was identical, and dinner was a small bowl of vegetable soup. I was issued with six supplements a day – and goodness knows what they were, as they were all labelled in German.

Worst of all, I was allocated a seat in the dining room next to a beautiful, slim and much younger Russian lady with whom I was unable to converse. Not because of any language barrier (she spoke perfect English) but because talking while eating was banned. As was reading, watching TV, checking your emails and so on. Instead, we were required to focus on masticating our food. At length. Not eating is hard enough for me . . . but not talking as well?

After about a week of this I was feeling so much better and so full of energy that the doctor suggested I see what he termed 'the mind doctor', the idea being that, once I had sorted out my physical issues, I should be sorting out everything else in my life. This doctor was essentially a therapist, and I confess I am not mad about the idea of therapy – it costs a lot of money, takes up time and I am never convinced it has results – but I dutifully went along, and she asked me to list all the things in my life that I wished I could sort out.

Pretty well top of the list came my mortgage. I had bought my house in 2008 and, four years later, I still had the same mortgage arrangements, which I knew were not ideal – not least because they were interest-only.

The mind doctor asked me why I hadn't sorted it out.

Because I had not had time, I replied.

I felt stupid even as I said it.

Back home, the Olympics over, I got straight on with switching my mortgage to a repayment one with a much better interest rate and a payment schedule that suited my earning pattern. This all saved me about £10,000 a year in cash requirements (I have a big mortgage). The only thing that had been preventing me from doing this earlier was my failure to find the time.

So even I, who writes weekly in a financial newspaper (and reads it daily), and runs a business that turns over millions of pounds a year, and has an MBA and a PhD in structured finance, even I find it difficult to stay on top of things and make enough time for my personal finances.

The lesson from this is that no one need feel ashamed for not having taken control of her finances to date, because it is never too late to start.

Being in control of your finances is an extraordinarily liberating feeling. Whether it is finally having a plan to repay your credit-card debt, or tracking down all your former pension schemes and working out how much more you need to add to them, or (like me) putting much better mortgage arrangements in place, you will feel a sense of satisfaction that you last experienced when you received a good school report, or the degree class you were hoping for. It's like finding that last piece of the jigsaw puzzle, or winning at Scrabble, or happening on a perfect view when out driving – an unexpected sense of achievement, secure in the knowledge that you have, through your own efforts, got to a place where you want to be.

I hope in this book to take you on a journey to that place, where the roadblocks in your life have been removed, and you are free to stop worrying and to move forward with all your other plans.

The barriers to getting there are not insurmountable. You won't need to do anything especially difficult to dismantle them. They are simply in your mind, and you need only invest some more of your time in order to overcome them.

So if you are wary of the world of finance, or feel a dire lack of control over your own affairs, or are very clued up but realize you may need some motivation to achieve more with your money, then this is the book for you.

I hope it will inspire you to invest more time and more effort into achieving your financial independence.

When you have, it will be your achievement, not anyone else's.

And it will feel great.

## CHAPTER 1

# YOUR FINANCIAL GOALS (or MONEY IS NOT BORING)

When it comes to finance, many people just switch off.

Don't do it!

Money can be interesting, and it can be fun. Honestly.

Even if you don't have very much of it.

Reading this book should help you to take charge of your finances and, as a result, you'll feel more confident and able to accomplish so much more. Yes, it will take some time and commitment on your part. But contrast that with the hours we often waste worrying about money, and you will see that the investment is worth it.

Different people will have different things in their life that they need to organize financially – they may be planning to buy a first house, or saving for a specific goal, or simply hoping to spend less money – but everyone, no matter who they are, will benefit from creating a financial plan. And especially women, of course.

Historically, a man might have been the only realistic financial plan we had available to us. But in the twenty-first century, sisters, we can – and we need to – do it for ourselves.

But before we proceed, let me put my cards on the table. I am not in any way, shape or form a financial adviser. I am not even a financial journalist. The closest my column in the *Weekend Financial Times* gets to discussing money is when I am found complaining about the cost of my waxing regime. (This is a serious matter, by the way. My pension planning budgets for regular visits to the beauty therapist, even when I am eighty plus.) But I don't usually tackle serious financial subjects.

What I am is a working mother with three children who are all, at the time of writing, financially dependent on me, which is why I refer to them as Cost Centres #1, #2 and #3. I have a mortgage at the age of fifty-one which, by rights, should have been paid off long ago, and I have a chronically underfunded pension.

And that's just for starters.

But I still enjoy the challenge of money, of using it to help me move forward in my business and my life, and I want to help you enjoy it too.

Money is not boring, and neither is it intimidating. So don't be intimidated.

My younger sister-in-law asked me the other day if I think I am intimidating. And I sincerely hope I'm not. But don't be intimidated by me, either.

Even if it looks like I know more about this than you.

It may be the case that I find money more interesting than you do right now, but that is going to change by the time you get to the end of this book. By the time you put it down, you will be a world-class expert on your own finances.

How will we achieve that?

I will show you all the things that I have done to master my own finances, and how I've made money work for me.

Because money is important for lots of reasons.

It is inextricably linked to bigger, sexier issues: confidence, family, fun, freedom. Money may not be – and, indeed, should not be – an end in itself. (As a head-hunter, I am always alarmed when candidates tell me all they are focused on is money.) But it is a means to getting to the place where you want to be.

It doesn't have to be about a bigger house, a car and stacks of jewellery. It may be about the founding and running of a successful and effective charity.

But everything needs money.

## Why women need to be better at financial planning

Why do we need a special book for women? Surely men, too, need to think about their financial finish line?

Indeed. But women have always taken a back seat when it comes to money.

Historically, we have earned less than men. We see the legacy of that in many modern marriages where men still take charge of all the financial planning. Women influence all the decisions, mind you – which car, which house, which holiday and so on – but once the decision has been made, it is frequently the man who arranges the mortgage, works out where the car finance will come from, or writes the cheque for the holiday.

But a sea change is coming. And for many households, it is already here.

Women are increasingly the breadwinners. In the very near future, more women will be the main earners in the household than not (if you include all those living on their own). And yet the women I know far too frequently outsource the financial decisions in their life to their partner, or their financial adviser, or even their father.

Are you one of those?

While professional advice is a good thing, you should know enough about your finances to know what questions to ask.

In my company, for example, I outsource all the information technology to a third-party provider who maintains our servers, installs our software, selects and orders our hardware and is in charge of our security. I couldn't actually do very much of that myself. But I know enough about it to be able to select that provider after grilling them about their methods and approach.

Before you work with a financial adviser, from a straightforward mortgage decision to a far more complicated pension plan, you should know enough about that too.

There are four very compelling reasons why women need to make sure they take control of their own financial future.

## *They live longer*

While the longevity gap is closing in the developed world, women still live longer than men, thanks to our extra X chromosome. Until it was made illegal under European Union law, life insurance companies priced this differential into their products, and women were at a disadvantage. But even with equal access to financial products, women still have to think more about how they are going to pay for what may be a very long retirement.

## *They may be on their own*

Astonishingly, I am still married to my husband after twenty-five years. But the odds are against us: government figures for England and Wales in 2011, published by the Office for National Statistics, showed that 40 per cent of women were on their own, many of whom had not planned to be.

When you get married, or move in with someone, you hope to stay together. And you certainly hope that your partner will not die before you. But this does happen.

Cath Kidston, founder of the eponymous high-street retailer, has spoken about how exposed her mother was when, after becoming completely dependent on Kidston's father, she was widowed at a relatively young age. The entrepreneur says that seeing her 'so vulnerable' was what gave her the motivation to set up her own multi-million-pound company.

Even if you are not on your own, the relationship may not be a source of financial security.

Jemima Khan, in a newspaper article published in 2013, pointed out that an estimated 70 to 75 per cent of Muslim marriages in the UK are not registered under the Marriage Act, meaning they are not legal. When the marriage is not registered and the relationship breaks down, the unregistered wife has no rights to spousal or child support and can even be left homeless. In the event of the husband's death, only the registered wife (and any children) will inherit.

## *They usually earn less*

Women in their fifties earn nearly a fifth less than men of the same age, according to a Trades Union Congress (TUC) analysis conducted in February 2013. Low pay and, therefore, the prospect of 'pensioner poverty' are major concerns for these women as they approach retirement. Women in this age group earn 18 per cent less per hour than a man of a similar age, which compares to a 10 per cent gender pay gap across the workforce as a whole.

Carolyn Saunders, a partner at international law firm Pinsent Masons, wrote in May 2013 in the *Guardian* about why women are losing out in retirement. Women are more likely than men to work part-time (around 76 per cent of part-time workers are female). They tend to have broken work histories and 'to work in service sectors where occupational pension provision has been less prevalent'. Currently, the UK's state pension system does not fully compensate the parent who deals with caring responsibilities.

Even the new system of auto-enrolment, whereby employers are required to provide employees with access to a workplace pension scheme and also to contribute to it, will exclude a disproportionately larger percentage of women than men. This is because the employer's duty to auto-enrol employees is restricted to employees with a specified minimum income.

At the time of writing, 69 per cent of women aged between sixty-five and sixty-nine receive less than the full basic state pension, compared with only 15 per cent of men.

### *They are increasingly earning more*

For the younger generation, it is increasingly the case that the major – indeed, sometimes the only – breadwinner in the household may be the woman. Over 2.2 million working mums are now breadwinners, a number that has almost doubled in the last fifteen years, which means that almost one in three of all working mothers with dependent children is now the primary breadwinner for her family.

This brings a whole new set of financial challenges.

If you are the one with the fourteen-hour day and the tedious commute, it is tempting to hand over everything administrative at home, including all the family finances, to the person who has more time.

But should you do that in blind faith?

This is your money, which you have worked hard for. You should know how it is being used, and be able to express a view on all key financial decisions.

## Identifying your financial finish line

Before you identify *how* you are going to sort out your finances, you first need to identify *what* you are aiming for.

Most people have very immediate and specific financial goals: become debt free by the age of thirty; save for a deposit on a house; buy a car. But before you get too bogged down in the immediate detail, start a list of your long-term financial goals. You can do this at any age, and your list will probably include some or all of the following.

- A mortgage-free home
- A fund to support the children's education
- A pension sufficient to live on in later life

Now, this may seem like the stuff of fantasy, but I promise you this is a worthwhile investment of your time – even if you are just twenty-one and leaving university, or (like me) fifty-one and very conscious that more of your working life has passed than lies ahead.

Next, you need to ask yourself some questions.

That house: where is it, and how much will it cost?

We all dream of some palatial mansion in the best part of town, or a magnificent country seat, but be realistic. Look into the cost of a house that you could happily live in for a while. If you are twenty-one, research the price of a two-bedroom flat somewhere. And if you are fifty-one, look for a house that you can envisage retiring to one day.

How many children do you ideally want to have?

I wanted six, reduced it to four after I had the first one and realized how knackering it was, and then reduced it to three once I realized how expensive they were.

And the pension?

Well, the lifetime limit in the UK – you can amass bigger savings, but they won't be as tax efficient – is not much more than £1 million. But even if you had saved that in your pension and were retiring right now, it would only buy you an annual pension of about £50,000. And you would pay tax on that.

You may still think we are in the realms of fantasy, and I do sympathize. No one does fantasy better than me. For example, I have never been thin, and I now weigh more than I ever have in my life. But that doesn't stop me planning for the day when I am several kilos lighter. What I don't envisage, though, is appearing on the catwalk during London Fashion Week, because while I could probably achieve meaningful weight loss if I applied my mind to it, the catwalk dream is never going to happen.

So, like the catwalk, thoughts of that house in Alderley Edge are clearly fantasy. But while the two-bedroom apartment in Salford Quays may look impossible right now, it should still be something you have on the list. You need to be realistic and rein in your wilder fantasies, but there's no need to dismiss what seems impossible right now. With good planning, it may be entirely possible at a later date.

And what about that £1 million-plus pension plan?

If you are twenty-one, if you assume that interest rates will average 4 per cent over your lifetime, and that you will carry on working until you are seventy (which, by the way, you may well have to), then you need to save £550 a month into your pension to achieve £1m. This will have you laughing already, I'm sure, as £550 a month is a fortune when you are twenty-one. But (a) if you are paying tax, then the government will contribute at least 25 per cent of that, so it is really £412.50, and (b) your employer is likely to be making some contribution, and (c) you will clearly pay more per month later in life, when you will be earning more. So starting off at £412.50 a month, while ideal, is not a do or die decision.

So you have your lifetime goals set out and noted.

Now what?

Now is the time to write down some of those nearer-term goals: the deposit for the flat you plan to rent to finally get you out of the parental home, or the car you want to buy, or simply the wish to be debt free.

## Before you get started

Whether or not you think you have your life sorted financially, there is probably more you could do to become fully in control. This is where you want to get to: the feeling that you are in charge of your finances, rather than your finances being in charge of you.

But where to start?

Information is power. The more you know about your finances, the more in control of them you will be. If your life feels like you never have any money for the things you would like to do, and the thought of setting any financial goals for yourself is laughable, then you probably think that knowing you are skint is all you need to know about your money.

Not true!

### *Do you really know how much you earn?*

Before you can fix your finances, you need to know exactly what they are.

Grab a sheet of paper (or open a blank page on a computer) and start to write down your financial CV.

How much do you earn per week, per year, per hour – it doesn't matter which time period you use. And do you know how much you earn after tax and other deductions, as well as what your salary is?

I encourage people to know not just how much they

are paid annually, but also to know how much they are paid on a daily basis. This helps to place a value on the things you are aiming for. It's not hard, and there are lots of online calculators that can help you work this out, such as www.thesalarycalculator.co.uk.

If, for example, you earn £25,000 a year, that translates as £96.15 a day or £76.23 a day after tax and national insurance (NI).

Are you really going to be better off for breaking your salary down like this?

Yes, you are, because it will help put things into context. If you know that your rent and utility bills come to £500 a month, then you know that you need to work a total of seven days to pay them.

## *Do you have any other income?*

I opened building society accounts for each of the Cost Centres when they were little. I paid in any money that they were given for Christmas and birthdays, as well as money from their grandparents and godparents. It's not a life-changing amount of money for any of them. But as they were growing up I taught them the concept of interest and interest rates by allowing them to take the interest out each year on their birthday to buy themselves a present.

In recent years, as interest rates have fallen to negligible amounts, they have barely been able to buy themselves a meal at McDonald's with the interest. And thus they have witnessed for themselves how falling rates have reduced the income available to savers. It has also taught them the value of shopping around for higher interest rates to increase the value of their annual spend.

So what about you? Do you have any savings anywhere?

If you do, list them. And also list the interest rate you are getting on them.

Some of you will have many investments. You may have property, shares and ISAs. The greater the number of sources of income, the more time you need to take to list them all. Make sure you do get to the bottom of all the detail concerning them.

## *What if your income is variable?*

I have a lot of variable income. In any one year I may make money from TV work, writing and speaking, but equally from none of those things, or maybe just one or two of them. You may get commissions, or bonuses, and so the exact amount you earn from year to year fluctuates. Plus you may get benefits that you don't recognize as income, such as private medical insurance.

So here is your next challenge – how much per year do HMRC think you have earned for the last few years?

If (like me) you have to file a tax return, do you know how much you earned in, say, each of the last three years?

My accountant, Don Fisher, who has been my personal accountant since I was twenty-five years old and signed my first book deal, files my tax returns. Yes, I send him the information he needs to compile them. And yes, he sends me the finished document to sign. But to be honest, the key figure I look at is how much tax I have to pay, and my actual income declared barely registers. But as someone who has a variable income, I should know what, at the very least, my last three tax returns say.

The equivalent, if you don't file a tax return – and most people don't have to – is your P60. There are over 30 million people of working age in the UK, but only about 10 million of them will have to file a tax return. If you are a company director (as I am), or self-employed, you will need to file a tax return. But most people who are working in a single job and paying tax through PAYE (i.e. the tax is deducted every month by their employer under Pay As You Earn) will receive a P60 form once a year from their employer.

Your P60 is the annual report made to HMRC by your employer on everything you have earned over the twelve months to the end of March, and it contains a full list of all deductions made.

So, can you lay your hands on, say, your last three P60s?

They will make for useful reading; you will be able to compare each year, like for like, with the previous year.

## *Do you know your outgoings?*

Knowing what your income is, and having it all written down somewhere, is a very, very good start to gaining control of your finances.

The next stage is to know what your outgoings are.

## The big things versus the little things

Sometimes it's the little things in life – that daily cup of coffee from a high-street chain, for instance – that are costing a lot of money. We will look at those in a later chapter. For now, let's focus on the big things for which you need to find money each month, including any debt repayment.

## Knowing everything about how much your home costs

You are probably thinking that knowing the cost of big items, such as your home, should all be relatively straightforward.

If you rent, then you will know how much your rent is. But do you know when your next rent review is? And how much notice you have to give on your house or flat?

If you own your home, then how much is the mortgage payment each month? Crucially, what interest rate are you paying? And if it is fixed, when does it expire? Is there a penalty clause that means if you change your mortgage, it will cost you?

Then there are the attendent bills: council tax, as well as utility bills. In each case, do you know how much they are costing? If you live in a shared house and share some of these expenses, do you know how much the overall bill is?

Typically, people only have a handle on the cost of the things that they are really interested in.

In my house, this means that Mr M has absolutely no idea how much our mortgage is costing, but he personally negotiated the satellite TV package. If I go away on business for any length of time, he will leave the post to pile up unopened, unless the envelope says something on the outside like: 'Warning! Your Sky Sports access may be cut off unless you open this envelope and action its contents.'

Just to show you how focused he is on certain key items of expenditure, let me share with you what happened when we last moved house, in 2008. I decided it would be better to manage without his physical presence and booked him on a three-day course to improve his golf swing at a specialist golf school in County Durham, hundreds of miles away. I worked really hard to ensure that on the day he returned, which was the day we moved in, I had unpacked our bedroom, made the bed, got all the TVs installed, and found the kettle, so that he came back to a lovely-looking house instead of total chaos.

As he walked through the front door, what do you think his first words were?

No, they were not, 'Darling, how amazing! You have clearly worked so hard to get the house even half functioning. It looks lovely!' The very first thing he said was, 'Have you managed to transfer the Setanta subscription?'

It turned out that his favourite Australian football team were playing live the next day. And the match was only available on some now-defunct channel.

To really take control, you need to get interested in how much everything costs you, including the duller elements. And yes, I agree, it can seem like pretty boring stuff. Plus it takes time.

We all only have 168 hours in the week, so why would we want to invest time in knowing exactly how much we are paying per kilowatt for our electricity?

But if you are reading this book, then you must be interested in setting yourself on the road to financial freedom. Getting to know the cost of your own life is a critical first step.

## *Do you delegate knowledge?*

Cost Centre #1 has been living in a house in Brighton for the last two years while he finishes his degree at the University of Sussex. He shares the house with four other boys, and one of them has a very organized mother. She has set up a bank account into which they each pay £500 a month, and then the rent and all the utility bills, including the wireless connection, are paid out of this account.

This fabulous organization has removed a big element of worry for me about whether bills will be paid on time. Plus the boys have been very good at keeping their power usage down. At the end of the first year of this arrangement, refunds were made as they had all over-contributed.

However, it has removed the need for Cost Centre #1 to know exactly how much everything costs. He knows that, as long as he sends £500 to a specified bank account each month, everything else will be taken care of.

Do you delegate financial knowledge in your home? Does your husband, or a parent, or a flatmate deal with everything financial?

If you have delegated financial knowledge, you have delegated a significant degree of control over your own life.

## Outsourcing can be good for you

Now, don't get me wrong, I am a great believer in outsourcing. None of us women would get anything done if we tried to do everything ourselves. Outsource financial *action*, sure. But if you outsource all the financial *information* in your life to someone else, you will never really have control of it.

### *Outsourcing tasks versus outsourcing knowledge*

It is one thing to outsource tasks, which releases you to focus on other things, and quite another to outsource knowledge.

Do you outsource too much financial knowledge in your life?

If you do, then it is definitely time to take it back. Start by interesting yourself in how much your electricity bill is, even if you get someone else to pay it.

Let's take the example of my bed sheets. I have a thing about thread count – the higher the better – and choose to sleep in sheets with 800 threads per inch. Washing these sheets is a total pain in the neck, and they need ironing, so I outsource them to the laundry. Just *my* sheets, mind you; the rest of the house can sleep in 200 threads per inch and have them washed at home. (If you are not careful, you can spoil children. It is like flying business class – my rule is that they can do that when they can pay for it themselves. Until then, even if I am flying at the front, they are flying at the back.)

What is the lesson of my sheets?

I know what I like, and how it has to be cared for. But the actual caring I leave to someone else.

## Resources

There is so much helpful information out there to help you spend less, earn more – and even learn more. At the back of this book you will find a section containing all the resources I refer to along the way. But there are two key websites that everyone who aspires to getting a grip of their finances should have on their favourites list.

The first is Which? (www.which.co.uk), the website of the Consumers' Association, the not-for-profit organization that looks into value. Access to this costs £1 for the first month and £9.95 per month thereafter and will probably save you that much and more every time you make a major purchase, from a fridge to a car to life insurance. You will find this website frequently referred to in the text, and I urge you to give it a go.

The second is a good financial comparison website. Personally, I use www.moneysavingexpert.com because I find it the most user-friendly, and I think Martin Lewis and his team know how to explain things easily. But there are others (www.moneysupermarket.com, www.gocompare.com and so on) and you should find one that works for you and bookmark it.

Arming yourself with these two resources will help you as you move through this book and want to see how to compare the prices of everything. The Which? website will help you with all the extra things you need to take into account when making any purchasing decision, such as reliability.

This book will give you a helping hand in mastering your money and using it to enable you to live the life you would really like to.

I will help you to set your priorities, to use your time effectively and to seize control of your finances and your life.

Whether you plan to take a week off work to tackle all my recommendations, or can only spare thirty minutes on a Saturday afternoon, this book will help you work out what is important and what you should do first, second and even last, to manage your money.

## Going for goal

1. Start your campaign to control your finances by spending some money. Invest in a notebook and call it your 'Financial Finish Line Notebook'.
2. Write down your financial goals: for the year ahead, the decade ahead, for the rest of your working life (or for the rest of your life, if you have already retired). Do them on three separate pages.
3. Write down your income (from all sources) and what you earn daily, weekly and hourly. Use the salary calculator I mentioned: www.thesalarycalculator.co.uk.
4. Move on to your major outgoings: mortgage or rent, all the bills associated with your home (council tax, utility bills), any debt repayment schedule, school fees and anything else that takes up a sizeable chunk of your income. Apart from being a useful exercise in developing your financial knowledge, these are the things that any lender (for example, the bank you hope will offer you a mortgage) asks for when assessing your ability to repay. So it will be very useful to have this information to hand in the future.

Have you finished all that?

Excellent. Then you are ready to assume control over your financial future.

CHAPTER 2

# CUTTING THE COST OF EVERYDAY LIFE

So now you have your main financial goals written down. How are you going to achieve them?

Nothing can be achieved without change.

That is true whether you have personal goals (for example, about your weight), career goals, or financial goals. The purpose of this book is to inspire you to ask yourself the right questions about your finances and then act on the answers.

And if you want to have more money to help you reach those financial goals faster, then one thing you could usefully do is spend less of it.

## Spending less money

If you are anything like me, you are probably thinking, 'How on earth could I possibly spend less?'

Most of us have cut back a lot over the last few years. Ever since the financial crisis of 2008 and the subsequent economic slowdown, prices have risen more quickly than wages, and 99 per cent of people have had to economize.

This chapter is not for the remaining 1 per cent. It is

for you. To help you think about what you spend, work out a way to spend less and challenge yourself to consider cutting back in areas of your life that perhaps you thought were sacrosanct.

I want you to examine every area of your daily life – from the journey you take to work to the time you go to sleep – and to ask yourself the same question about each one: 'Could I achieve the same thing and spend less?'

Learning to spend less is as challenging as learning to eat less. Personally, I find it very hard to eat less, as anyone who has seen me knows. Strangely, public comments about my weight (and there are many on Twitter) have never spurred me on to diet – not even the comment from the chap who observed that my backside was 'the size and shape of Paraguay'.

But if you want to achieve your financial goals, or achieve them faster, then learning to spend less is an important skill to develop.

## *Saying no is a financial asset*

I have always held the opinion that saying no is a tough thing to do. And women find it harder than men.

When I mentioned this to a friend, she pointed out that every time you say yes to something, you are in effect saying no to something else. Spending money is just like that.

No one has an unlimited amount of money, and even those people who do have lots of money need to make choices about what to do with it. The Bill & Melinda

Gates Foundation is trying to eradicate diseases, but it can't eradicate them all; its co-chairs and main benefactors, Bill and Melinda Gates, have had to choose where the money is spent. That will have meant deciding where it won't be spent, as well.

## *Changing small elements of behaviour*

There are so many daily habits that accumulate into big spending. By changing those habits and saying no to a few small things, you can make big savings.

I don't want to ruin the small treats you buy for yourself – I'm not saying that you shouldn't have a cappuccino each morning – but just be aware of what you are giving up in order to enjoy them.

For example, how much does a cappuccino cost? £2.50?

Multiply that by 5, then 4, then 12. Now you have the annual cost of your morning coffee: £600.

What could you buy with that?

If you smoke, giving up could save you even more money – not to mention the health benefits.

These decisions, small as they are, can change the course of your whole life.

Can you retire earlier? Can you support your children through university?

These small financial changes could have a big impact on your ability to make the important decisions in life.

Stephanie Nelson is the founder of CouponMom,

a US website that puts together coupons that you can print off and use, much like MyVoucherCodes in the UK. She was once asked on a TV show to calculate how much money she had saved. It added up to $85,000 over fifteen years.

'It's enough to send a kid to college for four years! It is real money,' she said.

## How I learned a lot more about spending less

In January 2011, I had a life-changing meeting in my office with Colette Foster. Colette is the managing director of Remarkable Television, and she is a remarkable woman. Remarkable is part of the TV production behemoth Endemol, and Colette is probably one of the most re-commissioned executive producers in UK television. The best way to describe her is focused. Very focused.

Colette was there to sound me out about co-presenting a new factual entertainment programme, to be called *SuperScrimpers*.

Surely there was some mistake?

I could hardly describe my own life as frugal. The previous year had seen me stage shows in both Edinburgh and New York, treating the audience to champagne before the show, while wearing jewellery worth tens of thousands of pounds created by Asprey. (Though, on reflection, the 'champagne' in Edinburgh was cut-price New Zealand fizz on special offer at Majestic, and the jewellery was borrowed. So maybe I am a natural superscrimper, after all?)

I found myself making the first TV series, which took twenty-seven days. By the time *SuperScrimpers* came to an end, in December 2013, I had appeared in four prime-time series, a daytime series and several special episodes created for specific times of the year (including Christmas) or for one of the various Channel 4 outlets.

I was very privileged at the advanced age of fifty to play a part in a successful TV series – although, between you and me, having a re-commissioned TV series is an experience akin to winning a pie-eating competition and finding that your prize is to eat more pies.

But it forced me to examine what we all spend money on, and how we might spend less. In this chapter, I am going to share with you some of the things that I have learned.

Here are the five basic rules for learning to live on less.

## *The first cut is the cheapest*

It is much wiser to make changes in your life while you are in control, rather than when you're down to your last few pounds. If your circumstances change unexpectedly – you may become unemployed, for instance – make some immediate changes to the amount you spend, even if you have been given a generous severance payment, or think you are going to get another job pretty quickly.

Don't wait until you run out of money.

It's far better to make the choice yourself than have it made for you when the money runs out.

## Saving money takes time

My Cleverest Girlfriend and Editor-in-Chief of *Money-Week*, Merryn Somerset Webb, has always believed this, and I have learned that it is true. Whatever you want to do more cheaply – buy electricity and gas, go on holiday, change your car, travel from A to B – it will take time to achieve it.

A simple rule is that you need to invest at least an hour a week in looking after your money.

## Information is key

Make sure you know exactly how much you owe on your credit cards and what interest you pay on them.

How big is your overdraft, and what interest rate do you pay on that?

Does your bank account have a fee attached?

Before even thinking about trying to save money, it is important to know what you currently spend money on.

You may be one of those people who know exactly what they spend on everything, and even work on spreadsheets in their spare time. But, of course, most of us are not – although, with a little organization, we could become very much better informed.

Here is one of my friends describing how she made sure that she had all the information she needed.

‘When times were tight for us at home, we decided to make a monthly list of outgoings. We itemized and averaged out every single recurring cost, from mortgage to childcare, right down to haircuts and petrol. Then we could see how much we had to spend each week on more discretionary stuff like food, going out and presents. We also had a board where we wrote every single thing we spent (of the discretionary stuff) so we could keep track each week – and then treat ourselves at the weekend!’

## *Making small lifestyle adjustments can often save you lots of money*

Remember the cappuccino example earlier?

Stephanie Kaplan, twenty-four years old and co-founder of *Her Campus* magazine, says she has friends who earn twice as much as she does. But they don’t have spare money to save, because they eat takeaways every night or buy coffee every morning.

‘They might make $60,000 to $100,000 per year but have no money saved because they’ve changed their lifestyle to spend up to what they earn,’ she explains.

### *There should be no sacred cows*

Are you spending money on something and can't really see how you are going to afford it for much longer, but you stubbornly don't want to give it up? A car, a holiday home, a horse, a child in private education?

It is tough to make the decision to stop spending money on certain things. This could have a tangible impact on your lifestyle, and it may set you at odds with your peer group. But there are times when you just have to do it, if you want to progress financially.

## Me and my reduced Cost Centres

For years we paid for our three children to attend the very best of the UK's private boarding schools. We never considered doing anything else; we had both been educated privately, in boarding school, and wanted our children to have what had been provided for us.

But then the financial crisis and the recession arrived, and we had to face the truth. We are neither Goldman Sachs partners nor in possession of trust funds set up by munificent grandparents to pay for school fees. Our children's education was being funded out of current income, and running a small business in a recession doesn't pay well.

The prospect of using up what savings we had, and/or borrowing money, made us stop and think, 'Why are we doing this? Will our children really be that much worse off in the state sector?'

There was also the local private day school, which does not usually admit pupils at 14+, and whose 13+ place we had turned down a while ago in favour of one of the grandest schools in the country. A letter explaining frankly why we had previously spurned them, and why we would be grateful for a further discussion, persuaded them to re-interview and re-examine our son. For £4,500 a term (as opposed to almost £12,000) he went to a school that sends almost a third of its pupils to Oxbridge each year, and where he made local friends (rather than ones who live in Moscow, or have a second home in Barbados).

The ten-year-old returned to the local village primary school after a three-year absence; again, a truthful letter to the new headmistress paved the way.

The boys were brilliant: the younger one was thrilled to be coming home from boarding school; and the older one, while very disappointed at leaving friends and a school where he was extremely happy, recognized that as a family we would be better off financially if he moved.

We had to adjust our lives and do more hands-on parenting. But that, too, was no bad thing. Our boys have probably lost their 'club membership' – Eton, for instance, is such a strong club that all the members now seem to be in the British Government. We shall have to compensate.

How will it turn out?

I have no idea, but I would cite two people who contacted me when I made our decision public. (That's the problem with having a national newspaper column. There are no secrets.)

The first is someone I know. 'I've always regarded private secondary education as absurdly expensive and, thank God, managed to put my two children through the grammar school system.' He did, however, pay for one of them, who had good GCSE grades, to do her A levels in the private sector. 'Just as I expected, this ended up simply being an expensive private members' club, and her results would have [probably] been just the same.'

The second is someone I have never met, a young man in his early twenties. His parents had done the same to him – removed him from one of the country's grandest boarding establishments and sent him to the local (and very much cheaper) private day school. 'I won't pretend the transition was all that easy. It was very difficult having my parents involved in my day-to-day education. But I made new and good friends (who lived around the corner, rather than in Paris, New York, etc.) and found that I really enjoyed the additional freedom I got from going to a day school.'

He got exceptional grades, and attended the university of his choice. He signed off his email with the reassuring comment, 'It'll be fine.'

And do you know what? I suspect it will be.

Contrary to some people's beliefs, private education – and especially the most expensive kind – is not necessarily the only option. I suspect the psychological barrier was, for us, by far the biggest obstacle to overcome. For our children, the transition was probably much easier.

The process has been cathartic. And while we acknowledge that others may not have as many choices as we do, the point of the story is this: anyone facing financial challenges should consider something they may previously have considered heresy.

## Identifying your cost-cutting targets

Cutting back on private education may be a million miles from the choices that you face yourself, but try to challenge yourself in every area of your life.

Let's take travel, for a start.

However you travel, could you do it more cheaply?

If you fly in business class, try economy. Go by train instead of plane. (Across Europe, look at the brilliant website The Man in Seat Sixty-One for deals and help with booking trains across borders.) Go by bus instead of train.

As you trade down the chain, and the level of discomfort and inconvenience grows, challenge yourself: do you really need to travel at all?

In 2001, we had the first of many 'staycations' where we stayed at home for two weeks, bought a trampoline and hired someone to cook and then wash up after lunch and dinner each day. I invited people over, stayed in bed late, had a real break and enjoyed the house that I hardly ever saw. The cost was far less than a two-week holiday for the five of us.

The first thing to do – before you try to do anything on a shoestring – is to find out how much you are spending on doing it now.

I find it very helpful to start saving by spending. So I suggest you buy a notebook and record, accurately, how much you spend (or use a spreadsheet). This is especially useful when you are approaching, for example, Christmas. Saving money takes time and effort; in order to get it back in your pocket, you're going to have to work for it.

Where are you spending too much?

This varies a lot by household, and identifying it is half the battle. There are marked differences in family spending between high- and low-income families. Research from the Office for National Statistics at the end of 2012 showed that the 10 per cent of households with the lowest incomes spent 23 per cent of their weekly outgoings on housing, fuel and power (compared with 8 per cent for the households with the highest incomes). A further 16 per cent of their money went on food and non-alcoholic drinks (compared with 8 per cent for the highest-income families). Only when it came to recreation and leisure was this in reverse.

So those earning the lowest salaries, who can least afford to be spending more than they need to on the basics, are doing just that. This was confirmed by Barnardo's *The Real Cost of Living* report, published in

April 2013, which revealed that poorer families spend up to 1.75 times as much as richer families (as a proportion of their weekly budget) on essentials such as fuel, energy and food.

Unsurprisingly, a Which? Quarterly Consumer Report in 2012 found that almost half of British consumers said they could not cope with any further unexpected costs, with 35 per cent already struggling on their current incomes. The study found that the top three consumer worries were:

- fuel prices (81 per cent)
- energy prices (78 per cent), and
- food prices (75 per cent).

So what are the areas of your life where you could cut back?

It's time to challenge yourself, as I said, in every area of your life.

I am now going to list a whole series of suggestions, but you could double them or treble them yourself. This list is an incentive to tackle your spending at every level, and at the same time to try to sweat your assets more.

I caution you, right now, that this list is not designed to be exhaustive. Those of you who want to learn 101 ways to use bicarbonate of soda will have to watch the reruns of *SuperScrimpers* (or buy their own rather charming book, which contains the tips shared on the programme by the thrifters who were recruited to appear alongside me).

Rather, this list is supposed to make you think about

examining every part of your life where you spend money – large or small.

## *Money costs money*

Could you pay less interest on your debt? Make an inventory of everything you owe, including a list of all your credit cards, in order of interest charged. And if you have savings, make a list of those too, and the interest/return you are currently getting.

### Cutting the cost of credit cards

In the first series of *SuperScrimpers* I worked with a lady in her forties who had few financial demands. Her children were grown up, she lived in her husband's house, she had a good part-time job at the local airport. But she had five credit cards, all with sizeable outstanding balances, and the cards ranged widely in how much interest they charged.

She set aside money from her wages each month to meet the minimum payments, and £200 more besides, while continuing to use the cards. But the additional payment above the minimum was made to a different card each month.

Why?

She told me she paid the extra back each month to the card she felt most guilty about using.

This approach was not very scientific – or even superscrimping – and I pointed out to her that she should focus her repayments exclusively on the card that charged the most interest (i.e. the card that was costing her the most money). Even better, cut that card up – and, indeed, three more – and only use one if she needed to.

How much are *your* credit cards costing *you*?

Could you cut back on interest payments?

If you are even a half-reasonable credit risk, there will be zero per cent offers out there, and also ones around 6 per cent. Proper, reputable high-street banks also offer loans to pay off credit-card debts, and I doubt they will charge you more than 10 per cent. Compare offers at www.moneysupermarket.com/credit-cards.

One of the cameramen I worked with on series one of *SuperScrimpers* saved several hundred pounds by doing this. Have a look at chapter four, where I discuss debt in more detail.

## Cutting the cost of your mortgage

Remortgaging usually costs money, in the form of fees. But if you can reduce your interest rate, then the maths can often pay off, with the savings made amounting to more than the fees charged.

First, get the facts together.

What mortgage rate do you pay? When does it expire? What rate could you get, if you remortgaged?

If you are borrowing more than £100,000 and you could save 1 per cent a year on your interest, then you can afford fees of up to £1,000 and still be better off.

## *Savings can be 'costing you money'*

By not getting as much interest as they should. Money forgone is just as much a waste as money unnecessarily spent. If you have savings, challenge yourself to make more from them than you did last year.

In early 2012, in the UK, almost two-thirds of adults said they switched banks to obtain a better interest rate on their savings. So don't be the odd one out.

If you have an ISA, great – it means that you are not paying tax on the interest – but ISAs pay hugely varying rates of interest, so make sure you shop around. Here is where websites like moneysavingexpert.com come into their own. Yes, it's a bit of a pain and takes a little time. But it is worth it.

All these little things add up, as we know.

## *Cutting costs in your home*

### TV/telephone/internet access

Most people that I interviewed for the programme were not getting the best rates for these. Consider restricting your TV subscription to the school holidays, or bundling all three together and moving to the cheapest offer. And don't be afraid to pick up the phone to your existing provider and ask for a better deal. Most providers have customer retention departments who are specially trained to deal with people planning to move and have authorization to offer them better deals.

If you don't ask, you won't get.

## Mobile phone charges

Most fixed contracts include a monthly package of free minutes and data use. Once that limit has been reached, the bill can soon rocket. So it's no wonder research has shown that the fear of accruing extra, often extortionate, costs when you go beyond your free minutes or data use is driving many people to take out contracts which are far bigger – and more expensive – than they actually need.

Check your bill out with www.mobilife.com or www.billmonitor.com to see what tariff you should really be on. And like remortgaging, if the savings are big enough, it may be worth finishing your contract early.

Don't estimate what you will use. Record your usage over the months, and let that inform the terms of your contract when it comes up for renewal.

Visit www.wandera.com and snappli.com to compress your data (and therefore your bills).

Visit www.techradar.com for advice on how to bring your usage down.

## Energy bills

First of all, check that your energy provider is not holding a lot of your cash. People who pay by direct debit usually build up a credit over the summer, or simply from their bills being overestimated.

One survey calculated that energy providers are benefiting from having £1.2 billion of customers' cash. One day we will all have smart meters, but in the meantime that £1.2 billion should, in my opinion, be returned to its rightful owners. Check your meter reading, call it in to your provider and then, if they owe you more than £100, ask for your money back.

We filmed doing this all day in Guildford, getting the occasional £100 back for people. A week later, my make-up artist, who had been hovering nearby, admitted to me shamefaced that she had gone home and checked, only to find herself £1,000 in credit!

Next, reduce your consumption.

One report found that UK households could save £40 million a year if they switched to the most energy-efficient appliances. You should expect to pay a little extra for more efficient appliances, but this will soon pay off. Check out their energy usage on www.which.co.uk before buying them.

If you want to set yourself the challenge of using less power, the nifty website www.imeasure.org.uk allows you to monitor your gas and electricity consumption, week by week. I have also bought an energy meter and placed it in the kitchen to demonstrate to the household – under their noses, and in real time – how much leaving on their bedroom lights and computers was costing.

And finally, of course, be ready to change provider. Comparison websites can show you which companies would be able to offer you a cheaper tariff (for example, www.uswitch.com).

Again, saving money takes time. You should review your energy provider each year – as you should every annual cost (insurance, for instance).

Put a date in your diary, and do it!

## *Cutting the cost of food*

The average cost of feeding a family of four (two adults, two children) in the UK is £50 a week. So if you are spending more than this, then give it some thought.

Sounds unlikely?

Just after our first *SuperScrimpers* series went to air, Sainsbury's published an advertisement showing how this could be achieved.

### Stick to a budget

In case you have forgotten, saving money takes time. To feed your household for less, do a two-week menu plan, draw up a shopping list to support it and then stick to the list.

Online supermarket shopping is good for this, because it is not as easy to be tempted with random purchases when you are on the internet. You focus on buying what you need, rather than what you fancy, and are less likely to be sucked in by two-for-one offers – or, worse, three-for-two offers – on items you won't get through. You waste less food and therefore less money.

Oh, and never go food shopping when you're hungry.

Challenge yourself to set a target and stick to it. This

will make the whole thing more fun. And it will be more satisfying when you achieve it!

Can you make soups, sauces and stews which can be used for several meals? Can you take packed lunches to work? Can you buy cheap punnets towards the end of the day on market stalls?

Alternatively, you may be inspired by one couple's commitment to buy food only from local, small shops and markets (at ayearwithoutsupermarkets.com). This has – possibly counter-intuitively – saved them money, because they have only bought what they want and haven't been sucked into buying endless offers.

### Use coupons

Stephanie Nelson, as previously mentioned, is the founder of CouponMom. She founded it thirteen years ago, when times were good and people were not looking to save money on food shopping. But she was encouraging people to use things like two-for-one offers and to donate the extra item to charity: 'We did publicity locally, working with schools and scout groups and teaching children how to buy food for charity.'

When the financial crisis hit, followed by the recession, there was an exponential growth in interest in her website.

The recession started at the beginning of 2008. At that time our website had been around for eight years, so we had been going for a long time and we had 200,000 members. Today, five years later, we are at 6.7 million members.

Are women more interested in saving money for groceries? The answer is yes – women make up about 94 per cent of our membership . . . The most popular coupons are coupons for cereal, although over half of them are for non-food items like personal care products, cosmetics, household cleaners and paper products.'

## Grow your own food

You won't save much money on fruit and vegetables that grow easily in a British climate unless you have a large plot and plenty of time, but it's fun. And if you have young children, it's an education as well.

No garden? Then grow herbs indoors – this can be more cost-effective.

## Learn to cook

I have discovered that many people eat more expensively than they need to because they don't know how to cook. Courses can be found cheaply and locally, usually by contacting your local further education college.

If you really want to stretch your culinary abilities, check out Jack Monroe's blog at agirlcalledjack.com. Jack is a single mother from Southend who set herself the challenge of feeding herself and her son on £10 a week. The blog contains various recipes and has accrued such a following that she also now has a book deal with Penguin. In an interview with the *Independent* she said, 'I have friends who have complained about not having enough money for food, but then they spend £5 on a convenience meal each night.'

The recipes on her blog are not only cheap but they are also delicious, as well as nutritious.

### Eat out for less

Coupons are good here, too, as are places where you can bring your own wine. Time spent researching both of these on the internet is time worth spending. Plus the swankiest restaurants (for example, the ones with Michelin stars) usually offer lunch menus for a fraction of the evening price. So for a special treat, without skipping a day at work, go for Saturday lunch and save a fortune.

Or become a mystery shopper, and review restaurants. You will get a free meal, and usually a small fee as well, for your time spent eating the meal and filling out the paperwork afterwards. Check out the website www.mystery-shoppers.co.uk.

## *Getting about*

Can you try to use your car less? Most of us feel ambivalent at best about public transport – especially when (as in London) much of the infrastructure was put in place a hundred years ago – but could you take the bus more often, or the train?

And if you have to use a car for commuting, shopping, or running the children to school, could you share with a colleague, neighbour or fellow parent?

Sure, it's not as convenient, but convenience has a

price. You may find someone to share with through the local networking website www.streetlife.com, or through www.blablacar.com.

Best of all, ask yourself, 'Do I really need a car?' What would be the real saving to you if you got rid of it?

Most people, if they added up the cost of maintenance, insurance, road tax, MOT and petrol, could pay for an awful lot of taxis instead. Or even rent a car when they wanted to go away for the weekend.

In many cities there are now cars that can be rented – even for an hour, to go to the supermarket. See www.zipcar.co.uk.

Public transport may be less convenient, but it is much cheaper! And not only that, instead of having to watch the road, you can use the time wisely. Try catching up on some reading, or listening to an educational podcast, perhaps?

Finally, why not buy a bike and get some exercise? Your employer may be able to help you arrange this tax free under the current government scheme, which would save you at least 25 per cent on the full price.

Of course, if you really want a car, there are ways to bring down the costs of servicing and maintaining it. An important one, if you're a woman, is to do some research – by which I mean ask your friends – regarding the likely costs of servicing and repairs. I say this because a study in the USA found that women were routinely being quoted higher prices than men. Only by demonstrating 'some apparent financial or mechanical acumen' were women offered the same rate.

Think it through.

Can you get a car that will cost you less money to run? What can you do to bring down the cost of insurance? (For instance, if your husband or partner is a better risk than you, then add him to the policy and see the premiums fall.)

## Cost Centre #1 gets a car

When Cost Centre #1 got a car, I insisted that hours of research were done because, as we know, time saves money. As a university student he has very little income, and he won't be earning much in his first job.

Why has he got a car anyway?

I am a great believer in incentive pay. So when Cost Centre #1 took himself off to a new university, after a false start elsewhere, I wanted to make sure that he pulled out all the stops for good grades. I bet him a new car that he couldn't achieve specific grades in his first-year exams. (I also believe that early success is another strong motivator for young people, but that's for another book sometime.)

To be honest, the grades I specified were high enough that I thought I was on to a winner. But as the year wore on, and it became apparent that I might have to actually buy the new car, I started to do some very serious research. He would have to bear the running costs, so they needed to be minimized.

In the end, I bought a diesel Mini. Here are the reasons why.

- It emits under 100g/km of $CO_2$ (which means it has no road tax).
- For the same reason, it is exempt from the congestion charge in central London.
- It does a lot of miles to the gallon, meaning that fuel expenditure will be minimized.
- According to trade data, it has one of the lowest depreciation rates.
- The annual servicing can be prepaid for five years, with great savings, and the service intervals are every two years or 20,000 miles.
- The insurance category was extremely low.

So six reasons why the running costs will be minimized in the future.

## *Got children?*

Justine Roberts, the charismatic and energetic co-founder and CEO of Mumsnet, has four children. She says that the evidence is that when money is tight, the last thing parents will sacrifice is the kids' stuff: 'Parents regularly shell out £700 on a buggy when they are struggling to have any luxury for themselves.'

But Mumsnet has lots of tips on cost savings for families operating on tight budgets, such as bulk buying and bulk cooking, home swaps, free outings for families.

What are her top tips?

'The key is to get organized; planning enables you to budget. I have learned pretty quickly what's worth spending money on – a Moses basket may well not be worth it (some babies like them and some don't) and a cashmere cardigan for a baby certainly isn't (although it's very nice to have). What babies actually need is really quite limited; try to separate the nice-to-haves from the necessities. You can also recycle a lot of things, and there are plenty of hand-me-downs about if you ask around.'

Entertaining children can also be very expensive, so challenge yourself in this area, too.

You will be astonished at how much is still available for free. When did you last visit your nearest library, for instance? There is usually a lot more there than just books (reading time for little ones, and computer training for bigger ones are just two examples).

One big-value way of entertaining families is by joining the National Trust. For a family with two adults paying by direct debit, this currently costs £73 and gives free entry to all their properties for a year. There are other organizations that run similar membership schemes, so do your research.

## *Buy men's items*

fact: in Denmark it's now illegal to charge more en's haircuts than for men's. In January 2013, sh Board of Equal Treatment decided that price es between men's and women's haircuts were effectively illegal. Their ruling came after a female customer complained about the price disparity of £41.35 for men but £51.01 for women (with an additional charge for long hair).

Are haircuts the only thing women routinely pay more for?

In 2011, a study was done in the USA on gender-based disparities between the costs of goods and services in the personal care industry. It found that women pay more than men for certain items and services – in particular, deodorant, haircuts and even the dry-cleaning of shirts that are no different from men's. The conclusion was that services and goods which contribute most obviously to the visible aspects of the 'gendered self' (such as haircuts, or feminine shirts) are most susceptible to price disparities.

So if you like the smell of men's deodorant, why not wear it? And do try to get your husband to pass off your dry-cleaning as his.

## *Get maintenance jobs done for free*

Learn to do jobs in the house instead of contracting them out. The big DIY chains offer courses on plumbing and many other skills, and these are free. Plus you can do them in the winter and stay warm at their expense.

Also, think of bartering as the new currency in the current economic climate. Always wanted that shelf put up, or that flower bed weeded? Ask your neighbour to do it, and offer to do his ironing in return!

If that makes you cringe, you could try your luck

with Justfortheloveofit (now part of www.streetbank.com), which offers skill-swapping with other people in your neighbourhood.

But if you decide that you want to test your newly learned skills from one of the above-mentioned courses, then the website ecomodo.com allows you to borrow stuff, including tools.

### *Going on holiday?*

Another staycation idea is to swap houses to save on accommodation costs. Try www.homelink.org.uk.

And did you know that if you order foreign currency online, and then collect it at the airport, you get much better rates and pay no commission?

## Spend wisely

As I said earlier, this list of possible economies is not supposed to be exhaustive. I want it to encourage you to go away and examine your own life.

Look carefully at what you spend money on. The list you could make is potentially endless.

When you do spend money, do so in a way that will allow you to save money in the future. When you are buying a house, or a car, or a fridge, think about how spending wisely will help you minimize future expenditure. When considering a house, the ongoing maintenance, potential energy bills and council tax payments should be more important factors in your decision-making than whether it has an en-suite bathroom.

And it won't be easy. The barrier to saving money may be you.

Emma Beddington has been a freelance journalist for six years but used to be a well-paid lawyer. The transition was hard.

‘I have definitely had to change my spending habits. I look at the row of €400 shoes that lines my office and think “that's six months' earnings now”. I spent so much on clothes and shoes when I was earning lawyer money. Stopping that hasn't been so much of a hardship, though – I think a lot of that spending was compensatory, a way of rewarding myself for doing a boring, unfulfilling job. I don't really feel the need for Louboutins any more, though I miss buying art.’

Emma also has two children.

‘On a day-to-day level, I probably haven't reduced my spending anything like as much as I should, though – I need to accept that books and cups of coffee and children's stuff also counts and that, if anything, it's that drip effect of €10 here and €15 there that has the most pernicious effect on my finances. That's hard, though, because it's a real lifestyle change – and anything that requires me to say “sorry, kids, I can't afford it” feels really difficult. When Christmas approaches, that comes with the queasy knowledge that I will spend too much and lose sleep over my finances in January.’

## Living life for less

If you really want to spend less money, then you need to allocate sufficient time to working on living more cheaply – not least, to allow yourself to overcome the psychological barriers. There may be more than you think, especially when it comes to trading down that statement car, or removing your children from private school, or doing your own cleaning. Often, the process of worrying about the impact of such a decision may be much worse than the consequences.

And remember that the smallest cutbacks can have a much bigger effect.

Think back to the start of this chapter, to the illustration of the cup of coffee. Giving up a daily treat to save about £2.50 can seem pointless if you are thousands of pounds in debt with seemingly no way out. But it adds up to a lot over a long period of time.

To encourage yourself, set weekly and monthly goals. And then reward yourself, if you achieve them.

---

I hope you will leave this chapter determined to take the first step towards spending less, which is to invest the time in gathering the information you need to start.

Work out the cost of your life. Then make it a project – a goal – to eliminate a proportion of it.

## The cutdown

1. Work out exactly how much it costs you to live. Start with all the big items – house, car, daily travel, utility bills, insurance and so on. Then move on to the smaller things. Write down each day for a week what you spent all day, and whether you paid in cash or used credit.
2. Try living on cash for a month, forcing yourself to get the money out of the cashpoint rather than using credit or debit cards.
3. Try spending no money at all for a day.
4. Go on a clothes diet. No new clothes at all (second-hand items from charity shops and eBay don't count) for a month, or even a year?
5. Set a date once a year to review all your annual expenditure.

## CHAPTER 3

# PROPERTY (or HOW TO SPEND A LOT OF MONEY)

Buying a house or flat, it almost goes without saying, is not something unique to women. But it used to be something that was very, very rare.

Point of trivia: if you were a married woman, up until the late 1800s, any assets had to be held in the name of your husband. In the UK, the Married Women's Property Acts of 1870, 1882 and 1893 gradually established the right of married women to own assets independently.

Single women were always able to own property. Even today, they seem more organized when it comes to buying their own property than single men. A Halifax report in July 2012 revealed that, in the UK, single women (62 per cent) are more likely than single men (53 per cent) to be homeowners. They are also more likely to own their homes outright (47 per cent against 30 per cent). I find this encouraging because, as we have seen in chapter one, we are more likely to end up alone in the future than we ever were in the past.

You are never too old or too young to have a property strategy.

In England and Wales you have to be eighteen to own a property in your own name, but there are numerous ways around that. So being a minor isn't an excuse. Mortgages are still available to people in their seventies – or, potentially, even beyond – if you can show evidence of the right amount of income.

Whatever your property strategy, and even if you already own your own home, it is worth reading this chapter and then tackling the homework section at the end.

## Should you be buying your home?

Just because we can buy property to live in ourselves, does it mean that we should?

So many people starting their career in today's financial climate despair of ever getting a foot on the property ladder. Even parents complain that it is very hard for their children to buy their first flat or house.

More and more people have to pay rent. At the beginning of 2013, around 31 per cent more households in Britain were renting than they were in 2007. And the number of homeowners had fallen 2 per cent over the same period.

I agree, buying property is hard, and for a number of reasons: mortgages are less easily available now; lenders require sizeable deposits; rent in London and other expensive cities is so high that saving for a deposit while paying for accommodation seems impossible to achieve.

But should we be expending energy and effort feeling depressed about this situation? Or should we just find a way round it?

## My property credentials

In 2002, I got a very welcome and unexpected offer to write a column in a new property supplement being launched by *The Times*. I was to write under a pseudonym, Mrs Moneybags, and the title of the column was to be 'How the other half lives'.

I wrote well over a hundred columns in this guise and, looking back on them now, wonder at some of the things I learned during that time.

Who knew, for example, that you could have a built-in shower for dogs?

Or that you could buy a horsebox with accommodation for both horses and people that cost more than some houses?

But this chapter is not going to tell you all about the properties I featured in my column back then. (If you would like to know where in London you can find property with a ballroom attached – or even, in the case of one property, two – they are all online.)

No, this chapter is going to make you think about buying and owning property yourself, rather than seeing it as an impossible dream. It will, I hope, resolve some questions. But frankly, if it does its job properly, by the end *you* are going to be the one who is coming up with the answers.

We are going to start by defining your property strategy. We'll look at whether renting is such a bad thing, and how you can make it more palatable, before considering whether a mortgage is affordable. We'll also weigh up the benefits of buying something that you don't live in.

And finally, I am going to try to share some things with you along the way to make sure that, if you do buy, you minimize the risks as far as possible.

## What is your property strategy?

So let's start with having a property strategy. You will need one of these not only to help you determine your financial finish line (see chapter one) but also to provide yourself with a handy answer any time someone (Mum or Dad?) asks you an annoying question about whether you are ever going to buy your own home.

My main property strategy would aim to ensure that I won't be paying rent during my retirement, and I recommend that you start with that in mind. This means that by the time you are sixty-five, say, or seventy (because more of us are going to have to work for longer), you don't want to have any money owing on your mortgage.

Let's say that, if you are going to take twenty-five years to pay off a mortgage, why not start when you are forty? By that time you may have saved a reasonable sum towards a deposit, and your parents – who, hopefully, will still be around – will be retired and will have a better idea of whether they can help you or not.

# Buy now or rent?

While there are any number of banks and organizations that are willing to lend money to someone who is buying their first property, almost all of them still have quite a number of requirements you will need to meet before they will do so. You will need a sizeable deposit (anywhere from 25 to 40 per cent), a job with a minimum level of regular income, and a strong credit record. (See the chapter on debt for how to make sure that your credit record is everything you wish it to be.)

Given all that, let's think about the key questions you may want to ask yourself before you go ahead.

## *Do you really need or want a mortgage?*

Is it really worth it?

In October 2012, the Which? Quarterly Consumer Report noted that the average household with a mortgage (around 35 per cent of the population) owes approximately £75,000, or a median of £49,000.

Lots of us can't cope with our mortgage, which begs the question: should we have one in the first place? Of the 85,035 homeowners who sought the help of the UK's national debt charity in 2011, 21 per cent were in arrears on their mortgage, and nearly half of them were women.

If you are a prospective first-time buyer and a young and ambitious woman, then you should consider how much flexibility you will be able to enjoy if you have a large mortgage on a property in, say, central London. Sure, if you are posted away from London, you could sell (would you really make money after you have sold?) or rent the property out (this is much more stressful than it sounds). But whichever way you look at it, a big mortgage could be a hindrance.

## *Is renting really such a bad alternative?*

The high barriers to first-time property purchase have led to considerably fewer mortgage approvals, which are currently running at only half of what they were at the height of the housing boom (in mid-2012, mortgage approvals fell to a fifteen-year low). This means that renting may well be the only option for many people.

But is that really a bad thing?

I have spoken to many young women about the 'buying versus renting' dilemma. So many of them tell me that they resent putting the money into someone else's pocket, instead of paying off their own mortgage.

But renting may be a way of keeping a lot more money in your own pocket. And at the same time you may increase your ability to earn money by being more mobile and flexible. I would argue for renting, for as long as possible, until your future is much more certain.

Put off the purchase until you have a better idea of whether or not you are going to get married or partner up with someone, and what their financial circumstances and career plans are, or are likely to be. You may, of course, have decided that you are not going to get married and are going to do it all by yourself. But even then, you may want to consider waiting a little while. You may decide that you want to have children, and may therefore need to consider settling close to the right schools.

## *Is buying more affordable than renting?*

You need to work out the sums. Lots of people think that buying is cheaper than renting, because mortgage rates are currently low.

Is that true?

There is a useful rough-and-ready calculator on the BBC website that will give you an idea of what a mortgage may cost you: http://www.bbc.co.uk/homes/property/mortgagecalculator.shtml. To start with, the cost of buying a property is not just the purchase price. There are a lot of other upfront costs as well.

What are they?

- *Tax on the purchase.* Unless you buy a property under £125,001, you will have to pay a tax called Stamp Duty, which increases as the value of the property increases.
- *Legal costs.* The legal process of transferring the ownership of a property from one person to another is known as conveyancing, and for most people (and for everyone requiring a mortgage) this is done by a lawyer. Unlike Stamp Duty, this should be negotiable, so shop around.

- *Mortgage arrangement fees.* Typically these can be around £1,000 or more, and if you can't afford them up front you will probably pay a higher interest rate on the mortgage.
- *Moving costs.* You can minimize these by renting your own van, and getting friends and family to help. But you can still count on there being some expense associated with moving into a property that you are buying. If you are currently renting a furnished property, and possess none of the basics, it will all add up. A bed? A washing machine?

So now the maths for renting versus buying looks like this.

| Assume | Buy | Rent |
|---|---|---|
| Cost of property | £400,000 | £0 |
| Cost of purchase (Stamp Duty, solicitor, mortgage arrangement fee) | £15,000 (has to be found from somewhere) | £0 |
| Deposit | £80,000 (also has to be found from somewhere) | Six weeks' rent that will be returned to you (make sure they put it in an interest-bearing account) |
| Borrow | £320,000 | £0 |

| Assume | Buy | Rent |
|---|---|---|
| Interest | 5 per cent | £0 (but you should be earning interest on your deposit) |
| Monthly payments – interest only | £1,333 (using the BBC calculator) | Rent – say £1,400 a month |
| Monthly payments – repayment | £1,850 | N/a |
| Maintenance (service charge, sinking fund, ground rent, emergency repairs) | ? (could be huge) | £0 – it is the landlord's responsibility |

## Can you afford to buy a big enough home?

If you buy, how much could you afford to pay on your mortgage?

Calculate how much rent you pay and, if this was a mortgage payment, what size of mortgage it would support. Here is a very simplistic way to do the sums.

- Multiply your rent by 12 to give you an annual rent.
- Choose your interest rate (use 5 per cent, if you can't be bothered to look one up).

- Multiply your annual rent by 100, and then divide by the interest rate.

If your rent is, say, £500 a month, then the maths is:

- 12 x £500 = £6,000
- £6,000 x 100 = £600,000
- £600,000 ÷ 5 = £120,000

So if you can afford to pay £500 a month in rent, you can afford to buy something worth £120,000 plus whatever deposit you can get together.

Between 2000 and 2008, I rented a house in the next village to where we live now. We had chosen to sell our home to invest all available cash into my business. Our rented house had four bedrooms, two reception rooms, eat-in kitchen, separate laundry room, outbuildings, a glorious one-acre garden, and it backed on to fields all round. The village is five minutes' drive from Didcot Parkway train station, which is forty-five minutes from London (with frequent trains). The rent, in 2000, was £1,200 a month. The property was worth about £850,000.

Back in 2000, I would have been lucky to get a mortgage with an interest rate of less than 6 per cent. On an interest-only basis, that would have cost me £51,000 a year, or £4,250 a month. Our annual rent (£14,400) would have supported an interest-only loan of £240,000. Even if the mortgage rate had fallen to 4 per cent, the amount I could have borrowed would have been nowhere near the value of the house.

And what if the roof suffered damage? Or the pipes burst? Or we discovered dry rot?

I didn't have to worry about all that, because I was not the owner. It was someone else's risk, and someone else's expense.

## If you rent somewhere, is it sometimes worth fixing up the place?

I know that people often resent renting, because they can't fix the property up to their satisfaction. After all, why improve the value of someone else's property?

But it may be possible to get the improvements you want. I have two suggestions to make, both of which I did.

One is to look at how long you are going to remain in the property, and work out the value to you of your improvement over that time.

- *Another six months?* Probably worth buying a new loo seat.
- *Another year?* Then the cost of the paint to redecorate the kitchen and your bedroom is almost certainly worth it for the enjoyment you will get out of it during that time.
- *Two more years?* If you can't stand the carpet, it is perfectly possible to find very cheap carpet.

For more major renovations I would try to come to a deal with the landlord.

After we had lived in the house for three years, we were getting frustrated with sharing the one bathroom with children (who were taking longer and longer in the shower), let alone any visitors. There was no door from the kitchen to the wonderful one-acre garden, and the kitchen cabinets were minimal, to say the least.

We cut a deal with the landlords that they would spend £40,000 on the property to give us a new kitchen and utility room, a repositioned back door and an en-suite bathroom. And we would agree to a rent increase of £300 a month, plus an automatic rent rise each year at the prevailing inflation rate.

Now, not all landlords are as enlightened or amenable, but I am trying to make the point that you should not automatically think that you (or your landlord) can't or shouldn't make improvements to a rented property.

You will need to ask your landlord before doing anything to the property. But don't hesitate to call up and try to negotiate over improvements.

Be positive! Take action!

## Still want to buy?

If I haven't put you off, and/or you are at an age and stage where buying is a sensible idea, then let's consider it carefully.

Most people would regard their house as the biggest single item they will ever buy, and it will usually involve taking on a massive amount of debt. If you have children, of course, this is not true (children may well end up costing you much more than a house). And yet, the decision to try to buy your first house as soon as possible is expected and almost taken for granted – even more so than throwing away the contraceptives and trying for a baby.

Both, in my view, will be big investments, and so both should be considered carefully.

Think back to your financial finish line. If your goal was to have a home with no mortgage by a certain age, then there is nothing to say that you have to start your journey towards that goal with a barely affordable, highly mortgaged property in central London.

Why not start with a more affordable and easily rented property in an area you know well? Say, the place where you grew up?

## Buying property you are not going to live in

Does this sound weird?

If you want to buy property as an investment, then do exactly that. Find somewhere where there is a demand for places to rent, where the rental income represents a proper yield, where property prices are affordable, where you can get to know the market and maybe have the support of family living nearby to manage the property. How about somewhere near your parents?

In early 2012, fourteen-year-old Willow Tufano bought her first property, jointly with her mother. It was a three-bedroom house in Port Charlotte, Florida, that cost US$24,000 and currently rents out for US$700 a month. Willow's plan (see, you can have a plan, even at fourteen) is to buy her mother out, using her share of the rent.

Okay, now here's the maths: mortgage rates in the USA are, at most, 5 per cent. So Willow's interest on her half of the mortgage will be no more than US$600 a year, and her rent from her half of the house will be US$4,200 a year. Even after paying the mortgage interest, she will have US$3,600 left over with which to pay her mother back. And she will own the house outright within a few years.

Obviously, not everyone can be in a position to buy property at that age. And it helps that Willow's mother is an estate agent, so she knows lots about the property market, and that you can buy houses so cheaply in parts of the USA.

But you get the picture. Buy something affordable, and then rent it out to pay off the mortgage over a pre-defined period.

## Janine and the Parisian purchase

Janine is a girlfriend of mine who worked for many years as a freelance journalist and, having a strong savings mentality, had managed to save up £80,000.

What to do with it?

In her own words, 'It wasn't earning much, and I didn't have a clue about how to invest it.'

She had a manageable mortgage, a tax-efficient savings plan, some shares and was up to the max on Premium Bonds (which she used to stash her tax money until she needed it). She had always liked Premium Bonds: the winnings are tax free, she found it ridiculously exciting to see even small cheques land on the doormat, it's easy to retrieve your money, there is a very slim but appealing chance of becoming a millionaire, and the returns weren't that bad. But, sadly, the Treasury has gradually cut the chances of winning to keep returns in line with other savings rates.

She looked into buying another flat, and had enough cash for a good deposit, but the buy-to-let rates were high, there wasn't much on the market in London that she could afford, and it all looked too daunting. She wasn't about to start playing the stock market, so the money sat in a savings account, where she forgot about it.

Then a Parisian friend mentioned that she had decided to sell her small studio apartment there, and suddenly Janine heard herself offering to buy it. This suited both parties: they knew and trusted each other; the transaction would be swift; and no estate agents were involved. The flat was tiny but in a great area and, though small, the studio was beautifully laid out, already furnished and tastefully decorated. Best of all, Janine could afford to buy the place for cash, so there were no mortgage complications.

The transaction was painless. Janine went to Paris on

the Eurostar to sign the papers, which included two documents she had never come across before: a certificate confirming that the lead levels in the paint in the apartment were within legal limits, and another reassuring her that there was no evidence of any termites in the building. Janine and her friend then went to La Coupole to celebrate, and after lunch she took the train back to London.

Ten years later, how does she feel about the investment?

'I still surprise myself when I remember that I own an apartment in Paris. I haven't seen it since I bought it, but it rents easily and is worth more than twice what I paid for it. I have had the same scrupulous letting agent since I bought it, who accounts for everything down to a cracked bathroom tile. Taxes are manageable, and I have a source of euros for holidays and business trips. A spur-of-the-moment investment, and a great home for my cash.'

## Buying property with other people

Most people will end up buying property with other people. This will usually be to make it affordable. And it is often because they have entered into a relationship with someone, or because they are buying with their parents – which they may do for any number of reasons, at any age.

I can't tell you if this is a good idea, or not. (Who knows if that gorgeous man you are in love with now will turn out to be a complete dickhead?) But what I can tell you is that, if you do buy property with other people, there is a very important question to ask. And a very important piece of paper to have.

The important question is *how* you are going to own the property with them.

In England and Wales, you have to choose one of two ways to legally hold the property with them.

- *Joint tenants*. This means that you own the property collectively, and if one of you dies the ownership of the property is automatically passed to the other one (or more).
- *Tenants in common*. This means that you own the property in common but have a pre-determined percentage of it, and that share can be sold to others, mortgaged in its own right or left to someone in your will.

Which is better?

Again, I can't tell you, because I don't know. And I can't predict the future, sadly.

But what I can tell you is that it is important to answer the question before you make the decision. There are important factors to take into account, whichever way you choose to go.

If you buy as joint tenants with someone (for example, your children), then you are offered no protection in the event of divorce or some other claim on the property. If you buy as tenants in common, you must remember to make a will!

If you are buying with your lifetime partner, and you are not married, then you may well wish to buy as joint tenants so that, if anything happens to your partner, regardless of whether they have made a will or not – and many people don't (see chapter ten) – you will inherit the property.

The all-important piece of paper that you should have is called 'a deed of trust', also known by various other names, including a 'declaration of trust and co-habitation', a 'trust deed', or a 'co-ownership agreement'. This is a legal agreement between the joint owners of the property.

There is no prescribed way of doing this, but things to consider including in the document are the amount each person has contributed towards the property, their share of the property, plus what happens if someone dies or wants to move out, or if there is a dispute about how to develop the property, or when to sell it. In other words, it is a document that reduces the risks involved in buying with someone else, and is aimed at protecting you.

## Stony broke with little or no deposit?

The first place most people think of turning to is the Bank of Mum and Dad. That is certainly what I did when I bought my first home in London, in Prince of Wales Drive, in 1985.

If you are fortunate enough to be able to borrow from your parents, then the bigger the deposit you can put down, the cheaper your mortgage will be. Crucially, this is not just because you are borrowing less, but it is because lenders charge higher interest rates on mortgages where the percentage of 'loan to value' – the percentage of the value of the house that the mortgage covers – is higher.

If you are borrowing 60 per cent of the purchase price, there will be several lower cost options. Borrow 75 per cent, and it will be getting more expensive. And at 85 per cent (or above) it becomes even more expensive, with very few options.

## *Borrowing money from other people to help with your deposit*

The first question to ask is this: how are you going to pay them back? Are you offering to repay the money, either over a period of time, or in a lump sum when you sell the property? Or are you proposing to give them a share in the property itself? You should seek legal advice on your options.

Your mortgage lender won't want anyone else to have a share in the property, but what you can do is come to an arrangement with your parents (or whoever) agreeing that, when the property is sold, you will give them a share of the proceeds after all the debt has been repaid.

It's a loose arrangement, and legally woolly, unless they register a formal claim to the property after you have bought it. This costs money, however, and requires the permission of whoever lent you the mortgage. So it's not usually worth bothering with – although, if you are the kind of person with very little responsibility, or if you co-own the property with someone your parents are unrelated to, then it may well be worth your parents doing that.

## *Borrowing from your employer*

If you borrow money from your employer, as long as they charge you interest (and it can be a very favourable rate), it does not count as a benefit in kind, and you won't be taxed on it. We can, and we do, help our staff with loans when they buy property.

## *Buying a new home*

There are lots of incentives to encourage you to buy a new property. Currently, you can do so with a 5 per cent deposit. If you already own a property, no deposit is required when you part exchange your current property.

## *Moving to a different part of the country where property is cheaper*

What do you do for a living?

Consider whether you could do it somewhere else where property is cheaper.

## *Finding a property with shared ownership*

This is not the same as buying with friends. It is a formal description of circumstances in which you buy a proportion of a property, and the remainder is owned by someone else (a housing association, for instance). You then pay rent for the part of the property that you don't own.

If you believe in housing as an investment, and/or you

see this as a cheaper or more stable way of providing you with a home than renting, it could be a solution. In parts of the country such as London and the south-east, people who are working in low-paid jobs may find that this is one of the few options available to them.

## *Help to Buy*

The UK government has created the Help to Buy scheme. The aim is to help people who only have a very small deposit, and who are looking to buy a property for up to £600,000.

Visit the website at www.helptobuy.org.uk for full details.

The scheme works in different ways.

### For people buying new homes

Help to Buy works as an equity loan scheme: the government loans you the extra money you need for the deposit and, when the property is sold, you repay whatever proportion of the sale price the loan represented.

For example, if you pay £200,000 for your home, and you borrow 10 per cent of the price from the government (i.e. £20,000), when you sell the property, you will have to pay back 10 per cent of the new sale price, not just £20,000.

The equity loan is interest free for the first five years. After that, you will pay an annual fee of 1.75 per cent, rising each year by the increase (if any) in the Retail Price Index (RPI) plus 1 per cent.

### For people buying older homes

Help to Buy works as a mortgage guarantee scheme: the government will guarantee the lender a proportion of your mortgage, which means that the lender will be prepared to lend you more (up to 95 per cent of the price of the house).

You still have to repay all the mortgage. And because the lender has to pay the government for the guarantee, it will be more expensive.

### Other housing options

There are other government schemes to help you become a homeowner, including:

- Right to Buy (for council tenants who have rented their home for more than five years and want to buy it), and
- New Buy (for people buying new-build homes worth up to £500,000).

## How to keep the buying price as low as possible

### *Buy from a friend, relative or a relative's estate*

This way you may be able to negotiate to buy the property for a price below what they could get on the open market. You can offer to buy it more quickly, and there won't be any estate agent's fees.

### *Buy at auction*

This is not for the faint-hearted. But there is a wealth of information available on the internet on how to go about it, if you're interested in doing it.

Personally, I have only bought property at auction in Australia, where it is the usual method of buying, and even then I outsourced the job to my younger sister-in-law. She, in turn, found it so nerve-wracking that she outsourced it to the husband of one of her best friends. (Auctions of any kind make me very nervous. I once bought a whole collection of *Wisden* – cricket reference books that the vast majority of people would find stupefyingly boring – at auction and found the process so stressful that I have never bought anything in person at auction again.)

You can find out about property auctions held near you at www.ukauctionlist.com. And there's a hugely helpful article by Lucy Alexander on property website Prime Location at www.primelocation.com/guides/buying/how-to-buy-a-property-at-auction/, which contains all the advice I would ever give anyone.

## Caroline buys a boat

Caroline Holtum, Sustainable Business Editor at the *Guardian*, lives on a houseboat. She and her husband couldn't decide where to live, didn't want to commit to London and were toying with the idea of being closer to nature and doing something a bit different. So they bought a boat.

'We thought we'd rather buy a boat outright than make the enormous financial commitment of putting a deposit down on a flat or house.'

They did the sensible thing of renting a boat first, in December 2009, and then bought theirs in the summer of 2010.

Is it likely to appreciate in value, like property in London seems to?

'The boat is likely to maintain its value, though not really to accrue any.'

Caroline's husband, Jamie, is a dyed-in-the-wool superscrimper and had originally thought the budget for their boat should be a maximum of £25,000.

'When we saw boats for this price, they were pretty basic. So I pushed for spending a little more. In the end, we got a nice one for £47,000. Jamie borrowed £14,000 from his mum, but otherwise we had enough savings to buy it outright.'

Those of you without a frugal husband and obliging mother-in-law may like to know that you can get mortgages on houseboats.

Caroline has clearly married someone who is very financially aware. He drew up a plan of how much they needed to build up their savings, repay his mother and cover maintenance costs, insurance and licence fees: £1,200 each month. The savings are invested tax-efficiently in ISAs. But Caroline remains fully informed – as per chapter one, she has delegated the practical aspects of the finance, not the information.

'He's put together a spreadsheet so I can see where everything is.'

## How to find the right mortgage for you

Having decided where you are going to buy and what, how do you know what is the right mortgage for you?

I don't want to repeat myself too many times, but I have to reiterate that I can't tell you what is right for you. What I can tell you is that picking the right mortgage can honestly look more daunting than picking the right husband. And there is probably a greater choice of mortgages than we will ever get of husbands – even if we look for one online.

### *Interest-only or repayment mortgage?*

Whatever mortgage you get, you need a plan to pay it off. Even if you can only afford an interest-only mortgage, one day the mortgage will have to be repaid. I would even go so far as to suggest that, if you are taking out an interest-only mortgage, then you probably can't afford to have a mortgage at all.

You should only get an interest-only mortgage if you know that your circumstances are going to change markedly in the future. I can see a newly qualified doctor or lawyer taking out an interest-only mortgage because they know they are, hopefully, going to earn a lot more in the future. Or you may know your Great-Aunt Agatha has made you the sole beneficiary of her will. Or you may know you are going to launch your dot.com business on the stock market in the next year for millions. Or you may have decided you are only going to own the property for a short period of time and will then either sell it or remortgage it.

But remember what an interest-only mortgage is – it is a bet on the housing market. If you are buying using an interest-only mortgage and property prices don't go up – or, even worse, go down – and Great-Aunt Agatha doesn't die and your dot.com collapses, you could end up no better off than you started. And, possibly, even worse off.

Given the expense involved in buying a property – see earlier in the chapter – if you sell it to repay the mortgage and the property has not risen in value, you will be worse off than when you started.

Are you a betting person? If you don't have a very good reason for having an interest-only mortgage, and you don't fancy betting on property prices, don't get an interest-only mortgage.

One acceptable reason for having an interest-only mortgage, in my view, is if you are borrowing the money to purchase a house you are not going to live in. Current tax rules allow you to deduct interest from rent received, but not from repayments. So if you are buying a property to rent out, then interest-only mortgages may be more palatable. But they are still a bet on the housing market.

Make sure you have a mortgage strategy so that you know how you are going to pay off the mortgage.

Because my income is very variable, I knew I would be able to save money but I didn't know whether I could do it on a regular monthly basis. So I took out an interest-only mortgage for three years and saved money into a separate account as and when I could. I then paid down a big chunk of the mortgage to get my loan-to-value percentage under 75 per cent. I was able to remortgage to a repayment mortgage with a much better rate (because I was only borrowing 75 per cent of the value of the property) to pay off the rest.

If you have the kind of income where you get bonuses or commission, say, quarterly, and these sums are reliable, then you could ask to have a mortgage where you make repayments quarterly.

## *Foreign currency mortgage?*

It is sometimes very tempting to borrow money in a currency other than the one in which you earn your money, or on which the asset's value is based, because the interest rates are lower. As I have said, this is not an exhaustive book on financial products. Rather, it is a book that is intended to make you stop and think.

So stop and think: if you borrow in another currency, and the currency moves against you, you may end up owing more than you borrowed.

## Borrow what you can afford to repay

Although I can't tell you what mortgage is right for you, what I can tell you is that you need to make sure you know how much you can afford to repay each month. Your Financial Finish Line Notebook (see chapter one's homework) will have helped you work out what this figure is.

I would almost always seek out the help of a specialist financial adviser or mortgage broker – and remember that you are their customer. Share your property strategy with them ('I want to spend £x and have paid it off in fifteen years' or 'I want to buy somewhere for the next five years, then sell up and move to the country and, in the meantime, pay back as little as possible'). They will usually charge you a fee. And they are usually also paid by the lending institution with whom they arrange your mortgage.

### *How to find a mortgage broker*

I found my original mortgage broker when I bought my first flat, back in 1985, by asking a friend for her recommendation. This is still my preferred way to find one.

However, another sensible way to approach it is to use the Which? Mortgage Advisers service, which is initially free of charge. An adviser talks you through everything that is on offer, including mortgages that you can only get direct from banks and building societies. (Banks and building societies would much prefer to sell to you direct, and not have to pay the mortgage broker, and so they offer products that may well be cheaper for you if you go direct.) You only pay a fee if you decide on a mortgage (at the time of writing, the fee is £199).

## *What to do if you are self-employed or have a widely varying income*

Are you self-employed, or (like me) are you someone with a very complicated pattern of income? My earnings come from three sources: my job, dividends from the company that I own and work for, and dividends from the company where my writing, speaking and performing work is contracted from.

The mortgage broker will be even more useful here, but it may also help to open an account with a private bank and ask them to help, which is what I did recently. Even people who are not particularly wealthy can bank with a private bank, if they have potentially lucrative careers (for example, lawyers, doctors and so on). Private bankers are very used to finding ways for people with variable and self-employed income to secure mortgages.

## Buy the right property

This is a subject that people have written whole books about, so I am not going to try this here. My job is to talk about the finance, not the property itself.

But I can tell you that a really useful checklist for home-buying, compiled by Patrick Collinson, Money Editor of the *Guardian*, is available online as a video and is well worth watching.

## Selling your property

Finally, a word on selling your property in a hurry.

If you really must sell your property as quickly as possible, for whatever reason – found yourself on Interpol's wanted list? Or about to go bankrupt? Or about to lose the house of your dreams that will save you a fortune on school fees because it is near excellent and free schools? – there are numerous companies around who will buy it (just as there are numerous used-car dealers who will pay cash for your car).

Indeed, many of the home builders that develop new houses and offer part exchange on them use these very same companies to help them get cash in the bank. There are lots of them, and they will offer you less than the property is worth. But if cash is absolutely critical, the three best-known and most established ones are Quick Move, PX Houses and PXS Properties.

Whatever your property strategy, there will be myriad ways to achieve it.

Do your research.

Think outside the box.

But, above all, don't cripple yourself with debt unnecessarily.

## HOMEWORK FOR INDEPENDENT WOMEN

### For everyone

In a page of your Financial Finish Line Notebook, make a note of your current property position.

This could range from 'own no property, would like to buy a flat' to 'own three properties and am thinking of buying another one as an investment'.

### If you have not yet bought a property

What is your property strategy going to be? Buy now and live in it, or buy now and don't live in it? Or don't buy now at all, and try to save money instead?

Work out what you may be able to borrow, and what deposit you will need. Then work out how you can get that deposit.

What are your savings plans? Do you need to increase your income? Could you go via one of the routes mentioned in this chapter and buy a property with a smaller deposit?

# If you already own a property

What is the interest rate, and what are the repayment terms on your mortgage? Over what time period are you paying it off? Could you do it faster?

Do you own your property jointly with one or more people? If so, are you joint tenants or tenants in common? If you are tenants in common, make sure everyone who has ownership (you included) has made a will. Do you know what will happen if they die?

If you own your property with other people, whether they live there or not, and you don't have a deed of trust, get one drawn up. You can download basic forms from the internet, go to a solicitor, or buy a bespoke form from this website for £150: www.deedoftrust.co.uk.

Know the cost of your mortgage (or mortgages) and, if it is a fixed rate, when the rate expires. Write that on a piece of paper and stick it up near where you sit when you pay your bills at home.

Should you remortgage to get a better rate? Do the maths and work it out. Even if there is a penalty when paying off your current mortgage, you may be able to get a much better rate elsewhere that will still make it worthwhile.

If you have an interest-only mortgage, how is it going to be repaid? Look to see what a repayment mortgage would cost you, if you switched to that.

CHAPTER 4

# DEALING WITH DEBT

John Paul Getty famously pointed out that debt is much tougher on the many who owe little, rather than on the few who owe a lot: 'If you owe the bank $100, that's your problem. If you owe the bank $100 million, that's the bank's problem.'

Debt is a fact of life.

On average, households in the UK owe about £6,000 in unsecured debt, and 43 per cent of households have borrowed money. Debt levels are at their highest since the 1980s, with Britain's households owing £1.5 trillion. And it is women and young people (aged between eighteen and twenty-nine) who have been reported as suffering from the highest levels of debt.

But debt can be a good thing, as well as a bad thing.

Investment debt (a mortgage, a student loan, a business loan) can move people's lives forward, just like microcredit in the developing world (the lending of small amounts of money at low interest to new businesses). I know you will always find people, especially of my parents' generation, who don't like borrowing money at all. But I am not sure that is practical – unless you were born with wealthy parents, or married a millionaire.

In practice, most of us will have to use credit at some point in our lives, so we may as well learn how to handle it properly.

This chapter is not about condemning debt. Rather, it should help people who have no debt but are thinking of borrowing money, as well as those who have borrowed it already and want to be more efficient about paying it back.

## Are women good at borrowing money?

Women are more risk-averse than men, so are less likely to borrow money. But they are much better at paying it back. Women the world over are seen as more responsible borrowers than men. They make up over 75 per cent of microcredit borrowers, because they are so much more reliable when it comes to paying off a loan.

In January 2013, an Indian financial services company, LIC Housing Finance, launched a scheme that was available for a limited time only whereby interest rates were 0.25 per cent lower if the property being bought was in the name of a woman. Why? Chief executive V. K. Sharma said that the company believed women were more reliable when it came to paying back debt.

' Based on our past data, you will be surprised to know that if the house is in the name of a lady, then home loan delinquency or default is virtually zero. Then we decided why not this [low interest rate] benefit be passed on to ladies. ’

He added that women had performed better than men in credit appraisal.

Women's responsible use of debt can transform lives. I had never heard of the town of Bethesda in Maryland before I wrote this book, but two of its more enterprising inhabitants, Robyn Nietert and Betsy Gordon, set up a not-for-profit organization called the Women's Microfinance Initiative in 2007 and gave the first loan, in January 2008, to women in a village in Kenya.

Six years on, WMI provides a comprehensive village-level microfinance programme for rural women in East Africa through ten loan hubs operating in Uganda, Kenya and Tanzania.

So far, they have a 100 per cent repayment rate.

What has been achieved speaks louder than any book could about the benefits of access to credit. WMI analysed 833 loans that they had made.

‘ Six months after receiving their loans, over 500 borrowers reported improvements in many facets of their lives. While 96 per cent lived on less than $2 a day before the loans, at six months, only 14 per cent did. All of the borrowers began saving money on a regular basis, with many saving as much per month as they had accumulated in total before the loans. ’

## Is credit ever really a good thing?

Borrowing can actually save money. It can change lives, at home and abroad, by making things much cheaper.

A solar lamp that lasts for years costs only £28 and could save rural households in Kenya (who spend 15 per cent of their average income on kerosene) a lot of money. But £28 is a lot of money in rural Kenya, and no one will lend it to them.

At home in the UK, those without access to credit from their electricity and gas supplier pay more for power – if you are not deemed creditworthy (or the people who lived in your house before you were not), then you will have to prepay for your electricity and gas.

This usually means that the people who can afford it least end up paying the most, because the best energy deals on the market aren't available to prepayment meter customers. In addition, older meters need to have their prices updated manually after price rises or falls, which can take months and means you could be left paying old rates and owing a lump sum, or paying too much.

## What would I borrow money for?

When you are borrowing money, the key question to ask is this. Am I borrowing this money for something I really need, or really want to do? Or is this just to fund my lifestyle?

I have borrowed money regularly. I have a mortgage on my house still, at the age of fifty-one, which is not ideal. But two of the things I have borrowed for have been very important and successful investments.

One of them was my MBA. I think of student loans, or loans for education, as a graduate tax. This means that people borrowing the money should be really, really sure that the qualification they are studying for will help them increase their earnings. Follow the advice in my careers book and pick the very best university you can get into, because the brand name affects your future earnings more than anything else. I borrowed the money to do my MBA at the London Business School (I was lucky enough to do an undergraduate degree at a university in the days when tuition was free, and I paid my PhD fees out of my income). I deliberately chose the business school that was the highest in the league tables in the UK.

I also borrowed money – rather a lot of it – to buy my business. £1.8 million, in fact. Some of that I 'borrowed' from the people I was buying the business from, in that they took IOUs for some of the money. But the rest I borrowed from a bank, and all of it had to be paid back. The discipline of paying it back was an important part of running the business.

Investment borrowing – to buy your education, your home, your business – is, in my opinion, a good use of credit.

So we are good at paying debt back, and some forms of credit are worthwhile and can even be used to create wealth. So far, so good. But there are also a lot of women who have borrowed money and have ended up letting it control their lives.

Are you one of these?

## Debt can turn nasty

In the UK and other parts of the developed world, easy access to credit appears to be diminishing people's life experiences, not enhancing them. Payplan, a debt management company based in Grantham that, unsurprisingly, is continuing to grow – and even made the *Sunday Times* best companies to work for list – thinks that aspiring to live a lifestyle beyond your means (succumbing to so-called 'lifestyle aspirations') is the reason why many women are tempted into debt.

The statistics are sobering: in 2012, 65,000 women in the UK went to Payplan for help and, increasingly, those women were single. Jason Eaves, Payplan's director, explains.

> ‘In 2012, we have seen a spike with women between the ages of forty and fifty coming to us, but overall the main growth since mid-2011 has been in the twenty to thirty age group. The average unsecured debt of these female clients is around £16,000.’

In the developed world, a lot of women have got into debt as a result of spending more than they needed to.

Why? Sometimes just to cheer themselves up, an activity we commonly refer to as 'retail therapy'.

A survey of 700 women by the University of Hertfordshire in 2009 found that the primary motivation for 79 per cent of women respondents to shop was to 'cheer themselves up'. This is emotional spending, and occurs particularly when relationships are not going well.

But there are other reasons too. Women and guilt is a familiar theme.

A 2011 study in the USA found that 67 per cent of women have felt guilty about a purchase. But women are also more likely to stay in a job they feel guilty about abandoning, or give someone money because they feel guilty about their situation. And they are more likely to bail out their exes, too.

I have no truck with women losing energy over feeling guilty (as I wrote in my previous careers book). In this case, don't do what you can't afford to out of guilt. Lending or giving someone money may be a nice gesture, but you'd be a far better friend or family member if you helped that person to set up a long-term financial plan. Perhaps *not* parting with any of your money may persuade them to do this?

JoAnneh Nagler is about the same age as me but lives somewhere much sunnier, in California. She is a debt coach who learned her professional skills the hard way, not least through her previous addiction to retail therapy.

‘I was a debt cycler – I would cycle in and out of debt. For example, I never bought clothing with cash my whole adult life. I thought of clothing as a reward, so I never set money aside for it and always bought it with my credit cards. The first time I bought clothing with cash – and came home with a blouse I loved and no guilt – I was elated!’

Sometimes women get into debt because they are taking on extra, new expenses, such as having a baby. Nearly a third of mothers end up £2,500 in the red while preparing for their new arrival. Apparently, one in ten mothers are forced by money worries to cut short precious time spent at home with their newborn. Almost six in ten (58 per cent) return to work due to debt and financial worries – just 14 per cent return because they want to continue their careers.

Evidently, financial preparation is key for any woman planning a family.

Check your company's policy on maternity leave. Calculate how much you will need in order to survive, and save money in readiness (see chapter eight for more on saving for the future). And last but not least, cut down on household bills and unnecessary expenses (see chapter two for tips on how to do this).

Debt can have a disastrous effect on a relationship. JoAnneh is testimony to that – although her story, at least, has a happy ending.

Debt played a huge role in the downfall of my relationship, too. My husband and I married, parted and divorced in large part over money pressure and debt. The debt had boxed us in, limited our choices, and we didn't see a way out except to part. Then we came back together fifteen years later and remarried with the promise never to use credit cards again. We have been together for six years and we are as happy as clams – with no debt. We don't use credit cards or engage in borrowing and have agreed that the only loan we will take out is a traditional secured loan for a house or a car.

If you do want to get divorced, debt can limit your choices. With debt to pay off, can you really afford to move out and live on your own? Debt could prevent you from leaving a deeply unsatisfactory relationship, which is another reason to make sure it is kept under control.

Debt can possibly also affect your health. JoAnneh told me a cautionary tale.

Friends of ours were sending their son to a very expensive private college, at $60,000 per year, and couldn't afford to pay for it, so they borrowed against their overpriced, undervalued house, and ran up their credit cards. Now the man has high blood pressure and the woman has just recovered from thyroid cancer. We need to realize that the stress of debt can have a role in making us sick, and then change our behaviour. Sacrificing our well-being to have more stuff or more prestige is just not going to pay health dividends in the end.

## Are you one of those people who have let debt get out of control?

If you already have debt, here's how to start getting your life back.

It is very likely that at least some of your debt will be on credit cards. So how can you stop them from taking over your life?

Yogeeta Mistry is an elegant, poised 38-year-old from Birmingham who got her first credit card at the age of eighteen. By the time she was thirty-two, she had run up £33,000 of debt, accumulated by massively overspending on shopping and holidays, in her words 'just for show'. Like many people, having a credit card felt like free money to Yogeeta – and she had five.

'I was just making minimum payments on the cards. I had £550 to £600 a month going out of my account on debt repayments.' She couldn't even afford to put petrol in the car. But there was a turning point where, she says, 'I kicked myself up the butt and said, "You need to get yourself out of this hole."'

If you have too much credit-card debt – indeed, if you have any at all – then you, too, need to kick yourself 'up the butt' and get yourself back on track. Develop a strategy and make repaying the most expensive debt in your life a priority.

Yogeeta took the seemingly (at thirty-two years old) drastic step of moving back in with her mother to save money while she cleared the debt. It took her three years of working hard and keeping the cost of going out to an absolute minimum to do so.

## *What is your credit-card repayment strategy?*

How many credit cards do you have? Including store cards?

Get them all out of your purse and put them in front of you. Now go and look up all the interest rates, then order them top to bottom in terms of what interest you pay.

If you have any store cards, they will be right at the top of the pile. Store cards are usually the costliest credit cards of all, and my advice is to avoid them if at all possible. Even if you have only one credit card, can you name the interest rate you are paying? Far too few of us know what rate we are paying, or how long it will take to pay off our cards if we make the minimum payment each month.

If you have expensive cards, the first thing to do – other than stop using them – is try to replace them with cheaper ones. At the time of writing, for example, the following charges apply.

- Topshop: 19.9 per cent
- Marks & Spencer: 16.9 per cent
- Miss Selfridge: 29.9 per cent
- Selfridges: 27.7 per cent

Challenge yourself to pay less for your debt. Even better, get rid of it altogether!

Apply for a cheaper credit card. But remember, not everyone will qualify for a zero per cent card and, even if you do, there may well be a transfer fee (meaning that it is not zero cost). Something called a 'life of balance card', which offers you a low rate and guarantees to keep that rate for as long as it takes you to pay off the balance transferred from a higher interest credit card, may well be a much more affordable option than your current cards.

Remember, too, that every time you apply for credit, it shows up on your credit record.

Big Brother really is watching you.

## Get your credit rating checked

You should do this before you borrow money, or try to borrow more.

When I was forty-six years old, I learned to fly an aeroplane. This is especially bizarre when you consider that I started doing so in 2008 and got my licence in 2009, two of the hardest years, economically speaking, in the history of my business and my family. I loved learning to fly and, even to this day, I try to fly myself to every appointment that I can. I caused despair in the production office of *SuperScrimpers*, who valiantly tried (and failed) to insure the risk of the 'talent' piloting herself to location.

The truth is, though, that I rarely fly myself to or from location. This is because the weather in the UK is dire, and making TV programmes is much harder work than it looks. Flying myself, tired and in bad weather, would be too great a risk even for me, and so I have a safety pilot, Wonderful Wayne. Forty this year, clever, charming and single – girls, apply here! – he is also endlessly patient. He happily took himself off to the cinema in random places such as Norwich while I chatted up people in the street, with camera crew in tow.

Wayne recently bought a new car, something he had researched and planned meticulously. He had also planned to borrow some of the money from the bank, at a very favourable interest rate, and the bank manager wanted to lend him the money. But Wayne failed the bank's credit checks and so ended up having to borrow the money at a much higher interest rate from the garage that was selling him the car.

Did he have a long string of debt defaults? Had he ever been bankrupt?

No, none of the above. He just had a very low credit rating with the main rating agencies.

Why was this?

There were two problems: the consistency of his postal address, and his lack of previous credit history. You may think that having never borrowed money would mean that you were a good bet for credit. But on the contrary, it is important to show that you can borrow money and then pay it back.

What about the address?

Wayne lives in a cottage on a farm, and the electoral roll address includes the name of the cottage, the name of the farm, the road it is on and the town. Wayne's address on his bills – his utilities, his mobile phone, his council tax – either did not have the cottage name or the farm name or sometimes the road, and *all three were needed*. (My own address sometimes has the name of the nearby town, sometimes does not.) You need the addresses on all your bills to match – exactly – what is on the electoral roll, if you are to get your credit score acceptably high.

Wayne has written to all of his service providers and got them to change his address (which proved harder than you may think) so that it exactly matches the electoral roll. And he has got a credit card with a low limit and is using it to buy the occasional meal or item of clothing. By paying the money back over two or three months he is showing that he can handle credit.

This is a lot of fuss and effort, but if it gets Wayne better access to cheaper credit in the future, it will have been well worth it. And it goes without saying that it makes not one jot of difference to how he flies a plane.

## My credit score

Now, Yogeeta's story mustn't put you off credit cards. Managed properly, they can provide you with flexibility and also improve your credit score. This means that, in the future, when you come to borrow money to buy a house or a car, you will be offered better rates.

Stephanie Kaplan, aged twenty-four, explains how one of her friends works in financial services and, although she has a credit card, is terrified of debt and so doesn't use it.

‘She spends everything on her debit card, which has a low credit limit. I put everything on my credit card and pay off the balance in full every month, and because I have done that I have a very good credit score. My friend isn't getting those benefits, because she is too scared to use her credit card.’

I paid to look at my credit score in April 2013. As I had hoped, it was very strong. The first thing that helped my credit score was my age. The risk of you defaulting on a credit agreement generally decreases with age, although it's not always a proportional relationship. But what this generally means is that when you are relatively young, your credit score is adversely affected by your age.

As you reach middle age, those extra years are starting to have a positive effect on your credit score. Your middle years are when you are typically at your most ‘credit active’. Statistics prove that in your early middle age you are best equipped to pay off your commitments as they fall due.

As you get older, the financial commitments that come from a growing family often represent a heavy drain on your disposable income, and your credit score will temporarily decrease.

In late middle age, once the nest is empty and income is peaking – typically, when you are between forty-five and fifty-five years of age (like me) – the impact of age on your credit score becomes positive again.

Only when you are nearing pensionable age does the positive effect start to lessen, as your income is typically reduced. Even though this may not accurately reflect your own circumstances, it is true for the significant majority. As with all elements of a properly derived credit scorecard, the impact of your age on your credit score is proven statistically from a very large sample of consumers.

I also benefit from having no court judgements related to debt against me. Court judgements have a very negative impact on credit scores, as they are a reliable predictor of future default. Their impact depends on the number of judgements recorded, the sums involved, and how recent they are.

I made sure I was on the electoral roll as soon as I moved into my current house, five years ago. Being listed on the electoral roll, and making sure the address is an exact match with all your bills, has a surprisingly large impact on your credit score, as we saw with Wayne. Statistical analysis of a large sample of consumers has shown that not being listed on the electoral roll is a strong indicator of an increased risk of bad debt.

Unlike Wayne, I have regularly borrowed money and

paid it back, and that long history of well-maintained accounts has had a very positive impact on my credit score. Having a good payment record is a tremendous asset. Even if you make the very occasional late payment – and late payments are seen on most credit files (as almost all of us, however good with money we are, forget to pay a bill at some point) – a good payment record will usually more than make up for it.

## Who can access your credit scores and credit history?

Banks and other organizations that share their data with credit rating agencies can, in turn, access your detailed scores. And you can too. But others can access a less detailed kind of report, called a Public Credit Report. These reports are provided by the credit reference agencies to more companies than any other type of credit report, and give much less detail.

A wide range of government agencies, companies, banks and lenders rely solely on PCRs. All government agencies, together with certain companies (including the Student Loans Company), use PCRs. They are not permitted to view your detailed credit history.

There can be big differences between the detailed credit scores that some lenders see and the information available to those that are only able to view PCRs. Usually, the more information that companies have, the more likely they are to decide in your favour, so organizations looking only at PCRs may take decisions against you. Also, all organizations that make searches for employment vetting purposes, or for tenant checking purposes, are only permitted to view your PCR.

## Top tips to understand and improve your credit score

- If you took out a student loan prior to 1998 and have defaulted at any point on repayments, this will show up on your credit rating. (More recent student loans do not show up – in other words, they don't 'count' – but then student loans are another kind of debt altogether. I would see them as more like a graduate tax – you don't even get away from them if you are made bankrupt. Only if they remain unpaid after thirty years are they finally written off, by which time you may be a write-off too!)
- Crazy about him/her? You need to find out far more about your partner than if they are STD free. Ask about your partner's credit history before you become a financial unit. And be sure to ask for any outdated links (for example, to an ex-partner) to be broken. If you decide to set up a joint account with a partner, or apply for a joint loan together, or engage in any other kind of joint financial transaction, most

lenders will take that partner's credit history into account when assessing yours.

- Big Brother is watching. Any organization that wishes to conduct a credit check on you must ask your permission, but you should be aware that some employers and landlords may want to conduct such checks. Employers may want to examine your integrity and, particularly if you are being hired for a role with a financial services company, a poor credit history may count against you. Have you been in arrears on your taxes and are applying for a role with HMRC? Forget it.
- Students should be aware that, even before they start their first job, credit checks can be important in an employer's eyes and will take into account things like keeping up with utility bills, rent, mobile-phone contract payments and, of course, credit-card or store-card payments. Fortunately for the Cost Centres, the Bank of Mum and Dad does not show up on credit checks.
- You should be aware that only applications, not quotes, for credit will appear on your credit footprint and that the outcome of the application – whether acceptance or refusal – is not recorded. However, a lender will infer from a number of repeated applications for credit that you have been unsuccessful, and this can count against you. Space out your credit applications and avoid making several applications close together.

- Use some credit on a regular basis, but we are talking about £50 or so. This is not an excuse to run up huge credit-card bills in the aim of improving your credit score! Never take on more than you can afford, and always pay off more than the minimum on your credit cards each month.
- Remember the story of Wayne, my single, eligible pilot. Make sure you register to vote at your current address and that the address exactly matches what is written on your bills. Lenders use the electoral register to confirm who you are.
- Once a year check up on yourself – everyone else does, so you need to as well! Buy your credit report and make sure everything is accurate and up to date. Query anything that isn't. It is important to explain any missed payments by adding a 'notice of correction' – a statement of up to 200 words.
- If you really want a good score, then learn what 'credit utilization' means and keep yours below 25 per cent. (This is available credit versus what you are actually using.) Also, credit scoring can look at the average age of your accounts, awarding extra points for long-standing relationships, so try not to chop and change all of your accounts on a regular basis.

## How to borrow money from the bank

If you are borrowing from the bank when times are tough, do everything you can yourself before going there. You need to develop a narrative and present it to the bank, and it needs to say, 'I am in challenging times and need your support.'

This doesn't mean going in and telling them that you have cancelled your second skiing holiday this year, or that you have decided to keep only one of your two racehorses. It means showing that you have done everything within your power to reduce your household expenditure. Take a list with you – or, better still, a spreadsheet.

It is also worth asking questions of the bank about their credit committee process. Different banks have different processes, and different approval limits. So ask how the decision will be made.

If the decision is just going to be down to a computer, then you need to make sure that your credit score is as good as it possibly can be. If, however (and this is the case in most banks for most loans), it is going to be an individual person's decision, then find out what they will base that decision on. Your local branch manager, for instance, may be able to authorize overdrafts of up to £1,000.

## Student debt and how to afford a university degree

Student debt is a relatively recent thing in the UK, and university fees were only introduced in 1998.

If you take out a loan to fund your university studies, you are bound by the terms of that loan. The terms are very generous, by the standards of other countries that run similar schemes, and in effect act as a graduate tax: 9 per cent of your gross earnings will be required by the Student Loans Company once your annual income reaches £21,000. After thirty years, the debt will be written off. So if you graduate at the age of twenty-two, you will have the loan forgiven when you are fifty-two, regardless of how much of it you have repaid.

Does this mean that you can't afford to go to university?

Lots of students have part-time jobs to help pay the bills while studying. But I would suggest that you consider doing it the other way round – work a full-time job and study part-time.

Until very recently it was only possible to take out a student loan in order to fund full-time education. But since 2012, student loans have been available for part-time education, meaning that you could continue in employment, and have your study funded by a loan on very favourable terms.

If you are in employment and want to study part-time,

an even more affordable way to finance your course is to ask your employer to pay. If they will not fund all or even part of the cost of the course, they may be prepared to pay for it up front and then recover the money from you each month over a specific time period by deducting it from your gross salary (a mechanism known as 'salary sacrifice').

This works well for both parties: you repay the loan out of your gross income (as with the Student Loans Company), which is much more affordable than repaying it out of your after-tax income; and your employer will be able to designate the course fees as training and will therefore not have to pay employer's national insurance (the UK's payroll tax, which costs the employer 13.8p for each pound they pay their employees). It is a win-win situation, and as applicable to firms employing four people as companies employing 4,000.

## *Is student loan debt a 'women's issue'?*

It appears that women put more of their wages towards paying off loans and debts than men – in no small part because women often receive lower wages. In the USA, 20 per cent of women, compared with 15 per cent of men, use more than 15 per cent of their take-home salaries to pay off educational debt.

Even with the same qualifications, women tend to take home less than their male equivalents across most professions. Because of this divide, women spend more time paying back their college loans than their male counterparts. This is another reason for women to negotiate their salaries.

## Consolidating your debt

If you have accumulated a lot of credit-card debt and/or other debts, consider putting them all together into one loan. Repaying that loan in manageable instalments is sensible, if you can discipline yourself to do that. And if you have a good credit rating, and the sums involved are not too high (say under £10,000), you should probably try your high street bank.

Remember the lady I mentioned in chapter two, who had credit-card borrowings on five different cards, and paid £200 more than the minimum monthly amount required between all five cards? She could have saved herself a fortune by going to Barclays, her high street bank, and consolidating them into an unsecured loan paid off over three years. She had a good job at the local airport, and had been a customer at the bank for twenty or more years. But she never thought to ask the bank.

Why? Because she thought it wasn't there 'for people like me'.

Women often have a sense of inferiority for no good reason.

## Borrowing from the people you owe money to

This year alone I have borrowed money from two organizations that I already owe money to. As I mentioned earlier, I also 'borrowed' some of the money I used to buy my company from the people who sold it to me.

Does that sound perverse?

The first organization that I borrowed from was the utility company who provide both the electricity and gas at my home. Thanks to two years of estimated bills – which is, in itself, something to be avoided (see chapter two on cutting the cost of everyday living) – our energy bill turned out to be far, far higher than we thought it was. The monthly payments we had been making were too low, which left us over £2,000 short of the sum that we owed the company.

Their proposal, which they sent me in a letter, was to raise our monthly repayments by £500 extra per month for four months until the sum was paid off. And it wasn't even presented as a proposal. The exact words were 'we shall be adjusting your payment to £x each month'.

Paying £500 extra each month to my energy supplier would have been very challenging for me and, while I didn't dispute the fact that I owed them more than £2,000, I didn't see the need to repay it so aggressively.

I called them up and asked for an instalment plan, which is basically an arrangement to pay them back over a fixed period of time.

The woman I spoke to could offer repayment plans for up to eighteen months – any longer than that required permission from her supervisor – so we went for eighteen months at £120 a month. Much better than £500. And it was interest free.

I know that it isn't just me who's been underpaying. Energy comparison site uSwitch published a survey in April 2013, which found that UK consumers owe an estimated £637 million to energy firms, a 6 per cent increase on 2012. More than 5 million households are now believed to owe their energy supplier money, compared to fewer than 4 million in 2012.

The other organization that I borrowed from was HMRC, to whom my company owed VAT money. We invoice clients, including VAT, and have to pay that VAT across at the end of the quarter, whether or not the client has already paid us. Clients these days are taking longer and longer to pay – in some cases over 100 days – which means we have occasionally had to pay the VAT before we have received the money. At one point last year, this got really bad.

What was my solution? Call HMRC and tell them.

They were very helpful, and arranged for us to pay the VAT in instalments as and when we received it.

So, in both cases, I went to the people I owed money to. I negotiated, in effect, to borrow the money from them. If you owe a large sum to one person or one organization, they are the best place to go to first. In both the above instances I paid no interest, or even a penalty fee, on the arrangements.

Women typically have less self-confidence than men, which is why calling up and negotiating with big energy companies and HMRC is something that they may find a worrying prospect. But I suspect that most of the anxiety lies in thinking about it. The person on the other end of the phone is just that – a person, like you or me. And everyone knows that times are tough.

## What about payday loans?

The payday loan industry has earned itself a lot of negative publicity through the extraordinarily high interest rates that it charges for its loans. Because they cost a lot of money, I regard these as an absolute last resort. Unfortunately, they are quite commonplace. In autumn 2012, Which? found that 800,000 households took out a payday loan (the same number of households took out a new credit or store card).

In practice, despite the avalanche of horrific stories about people borrowing, say, £200 and then losing their house, or similar, the average length of a loan from, for example, Wonga is only seventeen days. The average first-time loan is £180, and £257 for all other loans.

These companies have a place in society, and I refuse to jump on the bandwagon to condemn them. They provide a service that no one else does. But it really, really is a place of last resort – even after the last resorts I am going to describe – because of how much payday loans cost.

If you need a longer-term fix, then you need to consider other things first.

## What happens if things get really bad?

If you find yourself in a position where your debts are overwhelming, there is no way that you can afford to even pay the interest on them, and there is no sign of things getting better in the future, then it is time to consider some more drastic measures.

We are very fortunate in the UK in that there is a range of well-defined ways to help people whose debts are destroying them. However, the very mechanisms that are there to help people can also be a means of getting them further into debt. There are lots of debt management companies around who will offer to help people restructure their debt. But they charge for this, and the charges can make even the worst payday lenders look generous.

When deciding on how to manage your debts, there is a lot of free advice out there. So before you start, make that call to one of the following.

- Citizens Advice (www.citizensadvice.org.uk)
- National Debtline (www.nationaldebtline.co.uk)
- StepChange Debt Charity (www.stepchange.org)

- Debt Advice Foundation (www.debtadvicefoundation.org)
- Christians Against Poverty (www.capuk.org)

If you do move on to take professional advice or support, make sure you ask how much it is going to cost.

There are a range of options to help you deal with things when they become calamitous, most of which will affect your credit rating to varying degrees. This means they will affect your ability in the future to open a new bank account, get a loan, or buy on credit. Make sure you fully understand what you're getting into.

Here are the three main options (but please note that systems differ slightly between England and Wales, Northern Ireland and Scotland).

## *Individual Voluntary Arrangements*

If you are struggling with debt repayments of more than £15,000, an Individual Voluntary Arrangement (IVA) can offer you legal protection from creditors. (IVAs are available in England, Wales and Northern Ireland; the Protected Trust Deed in Scotland differs slightly.)

An IVA allows you to repay what you can afford, but it does not apply to all kinds of debt (for example, a mortgage, student loan or child support arrears). IVAs usually run over a five-year period, after which creditors are legally obliged to cancel all remaining debts. Once an IVA has been agreed, all charges and interest are frozen.

You can only get an IVA through an insolvency practitioner. If creditors holding more than 75 per cent of your debts agree to the IVA, it will start – regardless of the 25 per cent who objected. There are costs involved in getting an IVA: an initial set-up fee, as well as a handling fee each time you make a payment.

Insolvency practitioners can be found by visiting The Insolvency Service website.

Go to http://www.bis.gov.uk/insolvency and click on 'Find an Insolvency Practitioner'.

Why would you use an IVA, rather than declaring bankruptcy and getting rid of your debts? Well, if you own your house it may well be taken from you. And bankruptcy brings other restrictions, which may possibly affect your chance to work. So if you want to avoid bankruptcy, an IVA may be the solution.

## *Debt Management Plan*

A Debt Management Plan is an agreement between you and your creditors to pay all of your debts. (It only applies to unsecured debts, not to borrowings that have been guaranteed against your property or someone else's.)

You make regular payments to a licensed debt management company – be sure that it is licensed by finding one on the consumer credit register at http://www2.crw.gov.uk/pr/. The company then divides the money between your creditors. The idea is to prioritize your debts and focus on repaying priority debts (such as mortgages, tax and bills) over store-card debts, overdrafts and bank loans.

Some debt management companies will charge a set-up fee and/or a handling fee each time you make a payment. However, there are also charities and organizations that can arrange a Debt Management Plan for free.

This solution is really for people who need a lot more help sorting things out and who don't have anywhere else to turn.

## *Bankruptcy*

Bankruptcy is for those who cannot afford to pay off any of their debts.

In order to be made bankrupt, a court has to issue a bankruptcy order against you. You obtain this by applying to the court, because you're unable to pay your debts. Alternatively, your creditor(s) can apply to the court, if you owe them £750 or more.

It is important to realize that, even though you are usually freed from your bankruptcy after twelve months, your assets can be used to pay your debts. In addition, there are bankruptcy 'restrictions' (you cannot borrow more than £500 without telling the lender that you are bankrupt) and your details are put on a bankruptcy register.

Your petition for bankruptcy will cost you £525 plus £175 for court costs (if you're on income support, you may not have to pay this). Assets you can usually hold on to include items you need for work (tools, laptop, a vehicle) and household items such as clothing and furniture. But your home could be sold, if this is the only way to pay your debts.

Your accounts will be frozen, but you may be allowed access to money for basics such as food. And your partner's money in a joint account may also be released. You may also have to make monthly payments from your income, an arrangement called an 'income payments agreement', which can last for up to three years.

My issues with bankruptcy are mainly that it costs so much – and even if you are on benefits, it still costs money. Plus it comes with a pile of restrictions (about being a company director and so on), which may affect your ability to work.

But the one issue I don't have is the 'stigma' of bankruptcy. There is no such thing. Very famous people, including Kerry Katona, Martine McCutcheon and Shane Filan, have gone bankrupt (or had a business go bankrupt) at different times, and sometimes it really is the best way to put some disastrous financial decisions behind you and start again. I have occasionally given people the money they needed to go bankrupt, knowing it was the best present I could ever give them.

## Women and debt

History is on our side.

Until lending began to be formalized, in the first half of the nineteenth century, women were very active with credit and used it to facilitate daily life. Research has shown that the hunt for and use of credit enabled many women to get by, and a few to even flourish. And all this was in spite of the legal restrictions that prohibited married women from entering into contracts, which persisted for generations.

Back then it was money for stuff, rather than money for money. Pawning and pledging goods for ready cash was as commonplace between the sixteenth and eighteenth centuries as credit-card transactions are today. But in the first half of the nineteenth century, the formalization and regulation of credit came at a time when most economic functions began to be seen as male prerogatives.

Options narrowed for women of all classes.

Things are, of course, very different now. But in the USA, for example, it was only in 1974 that legislation was introduced granting equal access to credit for women. The Equal Credit Opportunity Act (ECOA) changed the way issuers regarded gender, among other things, when making their credit-granting decisions.

Women have historically been better with debt than men. Better at getting it, and better at using it.

So take charge of the use of credit and debt in your life, rather than letting it control you.

It is time to put yourself back in charge.

## HOMEWORK FOR INDEPENDENT WOMEN

# Debt, dealt with

1. Get your credit score and then work out how to improve it. See www.experian.co.uk or www.equifax.co.uk
2. List all your debt on one sheet, together with how much interest you are paying and what that costs you each year. For example:
   - mortgage
   - car loan
   - credit cards
   - overdraft
   - student debt.
3. Then work out how to get rid of the more expensive loans first.

CHAPTER 5

# GETTING FINANCIALLY LITERATE

I don't know what you got for your eighteenth birthday. Did it have a financial angle, at all?

I got a sewing machine, which I still have, and which did save me lots of money. I still have a photo of me at an undergraduate ball in Oxford, wearing a pink dress made on that sewing machine out of a pair of curtains I bought in a charity shop. (I went with a lawyer. I still know him. Why did I not marry him? Marrying a lawyer might have been very financially astute.)

I was told recently about a mother who bought her daughter a very unusual eighteenth birthday present – a weekend seminar with a reputable financial planner. My first thought was, 'What a boring birthday present!' But then I came to realize that it's not boring, because financial literacy is a critical part of anyone's life.

What is financial literacy?

Keeping accurate information about money is simply maths, not financial literacy.

Understanding whether you should make a purchase is financial literacy.

It is literacy, not maths, which transforms lives. Finance is the filter through which things operate, but the competencies you should be developing are critical thinking ('Should I buy this? What financial goals should I have?') and consciousness ('What am I spending/earning, and why?').

Financial literacy can affect your life in many different ways. It can affect how much of your money you keep, how well you can make it work for you, the lifestyle that you can afford to lead. In fact, your entire future – and that of your children, if you have any.

This whole book is aimed at improving your critical thinking and your consciousness when it comes to both earning and spending your own money. This chapter specifically looks at how you can increase your familiarity with the terminology, the opinions of others and the whole concept of money. The aim is to no longer find it a boring or inaccessible subject but, instead, something that informs your life decisions.

We will look at why financial literacy is important, and I will make practical suggestions about how to improve your own financial literacy.

## Why is financial literacy important?

There is a whole heap of studies on this subject – and I have looked them up, so you don't have to.

People with low financial literacy are:

- more likely to have problems with debt
- less likely to participate in the stock market
- less likely to choose investments with lower fees

- less likely to accumulate wealth and manage wealth effectively
- less likely to plan for retirement.

Financial literacy is critical for promoting access to finance, and for creating an environment in which positive financial behaviour (saving, budgeting, or using credit wisely) will flourish. The OECD's financial education programmes for developing countries cover topics such as budgeting, saving, managing credit and learning to negotiate. These are all vital 'basics' for women in developed countries too!

Women seem to be hesitant to talk about financial matters with their friends and peers, which means, amongst other things, that they may be less aware of whether their salaries measure up. Financial advisers say many women need to be prompted to evaluate whether they're being paid what they're worth.

Experts say that many women simply aren't as confident and knowledgeable about financial matters as men. This applies even when women handle their family's household budget, including paying bills and making many of the purchasing decisions.

The Personal Finance Education Group, a finance education charity, has been calling for compulsory personal finance education in schools for a number of years. It says young people must be able to manage their money 'with confidence'. This view is supported by the founder of MoneySavingExpert.com, Martin Lewis, who has referred to the UK as a 'financially illiterate' nation – he, too, is pushing for personal finance and consumer rights education in schools.

## Financial literacy is important for every woman, whatever you do

Jude Kelly is the talented and award-winning Artistic Director of the Southbank Centre. She has worked as an artistic director since the age of twenty-two, and has been at the Southbank Centre for several years. Although she has never had to prepare the detailed accounts for any of the organizations she has run (because there has been a financial professional to do that), she has always had to take responsibility for the solvency and financial management of the organization: 'The buck stops with me.'

As a teenager, she failed Maths O-Level three times.

' But this didn't deter me, and it hasn't made me scared of big numbers or money. It shouldn't stop people. Once you know why you need to look at figures, what they apply to, then you can do it. '

She is right – just because maths was a weaker subject for you at school, this does not mean that you can't become financially literate. As Jude explains, Maths didn't capture her imagination.

' The problem with a pure subject like Maths is that patterns and results are not applied to anything. If somebody had asked me when I was ten to imagine a theatre company and how I would balance the books, I would have got cracking there and then ... I have always wanted to work in the theatre. Every production has a sizeable budget, and the production team need to keep an eye on what is being spent. But as director you've got to make the decisions around how to juggle the money to stay on budget. Financial literacy is a method to achieve what you want. ’

She cites the example of a thirteen-year-old boy who was fascinated by cars and wasn't interested in school. He was supported by a scheme called Outsider on a placement in a garage where he could spend all day with cars, but he had to learn how to balance the books. Within two years he was doing all of the company's VAT: 'More people could approach financial professionals to mentor them – I am sure they would be more than delighted to volunteer.'

## Things you can do to help your financial literacy

If you have followed all my advice in this book and know what you are earning, what you are spending, where all your savings are, what interest rates they are earning and whether you could get a better mortgage, then you are probably very financially literate already. But even then, I would recommend that you increase your reading more widely to include business finance, as well as personal finance articles.

## *MoneyWeek*

Start by subscribing to *MoneyWeek*. This is a weekly round-up of the world's best financial media, the Editor-in-Chief of which is Merryn Somerset Webb. Known in my *FT* column as My Cleverest Girlfriend, Merryn is one of the most successful personal finance journalists in the UK (also younger than me, more beautiful than me, in better shape than me, earned a first at Cambridge, speaks fluent Japanese . . . you get the picture). Her magazine, fortunately for me and many others, is aimed at making the world of money accessible to people without firsts from Cambridge. In very little time you can get a world view of the things you need to know about money that week.

Readers of this book can take advantage of a special offer: a three-week free trial and then 56 per cent off the cover price. Visit the website and click on the link at MoneyWeek.com/Heather to start your subscription.

## *Financial Times*

When you have read *MoneyWeek* for a few weeks, learn to read the *Financial Times*. Merryn writes for this also, in the 'Money' section on Saturdays.

I understand that learning to read the *FT* may not be a very appealing prospect – after all, we are talking about a paper that many would assume is dry and boring. But, like the subject of money itself, it is far from dry and boring. And (okay, I am biased) it is widely respected, including among the journalistic community, as one of the best written, most impartial and most interesting newspapers in the world. I agree with that judgement, and challenge you to take my four-week course in how to read the paper. And then we'll see if you agree too.

## Teach yourself to read the *FT* – in four weeks

It is always good to start with the print edition, if you can. Not only is it different in layout to the online edition, but carrying it around with you makes a positive statement about your financial literacy.

- *Week one (every day)*: read the summaries on the left-hand side of the front pages of both sections, and one article in 'Lex', the section which the very best writers work on, commenting on the business issues of the day from all over the world. Plus one named columnist a day: good places to start include Lucy Kellaway, Janan Ganesh, John Gapper, Michael Skapinker, Andrew Hill, Gillian Tett (start with her Saturday column) and Tim Harford. Oh, and me, of course, online.
- *Week two*: as week one, but increase the number of 'Lex' articles to two.
- *Week three*: as week two, except that you should also pick a piece about a specific company to read each day. In the paper edition, look in the index on

the front of the second section; if you are reading the *FT* online, select 'companies' and then pick a sector (for example, 'pharmaceutical') before looking to see what seems interesting. Or type the name of the company you would like to know more about into the search function.

- *Week four*: as week three, but add one piece from the editorial each day (in the print edition this is on the page with the letters, and the letters are worth a glance also; online, the editorial is a subheading under 'Comment').

After four weeks, I predict you will find it so interesting that you will want to continue and take out a subscription, which is by far the cheapest way to buy the *Financial Times*. (Make sure you also go online and set up alerts for companies you are interested in – your employer, perhaps, or that of your boyfriend/parent/partner.)

If you still find it indigestible after four weeks, having followed my prescription to the letter, then maybe financial and business topics are genuinely not for you.

## *The Economist*

Start by reading the summary pages 'The Week in Politics' and 'The Week in Business'. Then go through the index and pick out two articles a week plus one book review and the obituary (they only have one per issue).

## *Pick a company each month to study*

Read its annual report (all public companies will post these on their website). Why not start with your employer, or your company's biggest client or supplier? And if you know all that, why not move on to one of your competitors?

It will be much more interesting if it is a company you know, even if you understand only the most basic things about it.

## *Go and do a course*

I'm known for my enthusiasm for Finance Talking, a training company run by Miranda Lane that has some excellent courses (including many delivered online) called 'Finance Courses for Non-Financial People'.

Visit their website – and if you don't know which course to pick, email miranda@financetalking.com and ask her!

## *Join or set up a club to invest in stocks and shares*

In addition to offering an opportunity to make saving money more interesting, a shares club can really help you to become more financially literate.

There are 12,000 of these in the UK, according to ProShare, a not-for-profit organization that promotes share ownership in the UK. You don't need to be a financial expert, and you can each invest a very small amount of money each month. But by meeting on a regular basis to discuss your potential and actual investments, your understanding of the finances of companies will grow.

### *Educate your children (and yourself at the same time)*

Darrah Brustein is a young entrepreneur who has developed a series of books for young children to educate them about money. If you have young children, why not start reading them the series? It is called *Finance Whiz Kids*.

## Supporting behaviour change

Finally, I was reading recently about the Department for International Development's Financial Education Fund, established to support educational projects aimed at helping African citizens increase their financial knowledge and ability (with grants of up to £0.25 million available). In my view, it could be usefully replicated domestically to improve financial literacy.

The 'key elements' are:

- knowledge (of personal financial management, money concepts and financial services)

- skills (i.e. the ability to apply knowledge in the use of financial services and financial management)
- attitudes (including confidence, trust and personal perceptions about the use of financial services)
- behaviour (the ultimate objective of financial education being behaviour change).

And that says it all, really.

You should aim to become more financially literate, with the aim of behaviour change.

# Become financially literate

The purpose of this homework section is to help you become more financially literate in general, not just to know more about personal finance.

## *Start reading more widely*

- Subscribe to *MoneyWeek* and take advantage of the special offer available to readers of this book: a three-week free trial and then 56 per cent off the cover price.
  Visit the website and click on the link at MoneyWeek.com/Heather to start your subscription.
- Follow Merryn Somerset Webb on Twitter @MerrynSW.
- Subscribe to the *Financial Times* and/or *The Economist* (both of these have special introductory offers). If you want directions to selected reading, follow Lionel Barber, the Editor of the *FT*, on Twitter @barberlionel.
- Start reading the personal finance section in a Saturday or Sunday newspaper.

## *Do a course*

- Book yourself on to an e-learning course with Finance Talking (or a similar training company).

These are courses that help people in non-financial jobs understand what is going on around them.

- If you work in a bank, investigate e-learning courses in financial literacy – there is nothing more frustrating than working in, say, human resources or purchasing and not actually understanding how the company makes its money.
- If you are more ambitious, have a look at e-learning from some of the best professors of finance in the world.
  The website www.academictrader.org was developed after the 2008 financial crisis to make financial literacy available to all.
  The website http://alison.com/ has an excellent course in financial literacy at the personal level (but be aware that it is tailored to the USA).

## *Qualify in finance*

Consider doing a formal financial qualification, and make money your source of income.

- If you are going to do this while working, the best one to try out is CIMA. This allows access at any level (from A levels onwards) and is a very practical qualification.
  Visit the website at www.cimaglobal.com to find out more about the Chartered Institute of Management Accountants.

- You can also look at an ACCA, which will make you a Chartered Certified Accountant.
  Visit the website at http://www2.accaglobal.com/uk/ to find out more.
- You may even want to consider a CFA, which is the qualification that professional investors pursue.
  Visit the website at www.cfainstitute.org to find out more about the programmes offered by the CFA Institute.

## CHAPTER 6

# EARNING MORE

Most diet books can probably be summed up by the phrase 'eat less, move more'. This book, I like to think, can be summed up as 'spend less, earn more'.

This chapter directly focuses on making sure that you maximize your income.

There are many things that can increase your wealth – investing wisely, buying property, marrying (and divorcing) well – but this chapter focuses on earning as much as you can.

Two people I admire – yet probably never thought I would mention in the same breath – are Sir Winston Churchill and Nancy Dell'Olio. I admire them for different reasons, but there is one thing they have in common, and that is their response to needing more money. Both of them have demonstrated that their response to wanting/needing more money was always to go and earn it by writing another book, or doing another deal.

Nancy was my guest on stage in Edinburgh when I did a festival chat show focusing on money. What was her response to my question about how much money Sven-Göran Eriksson had finally settled on her?

'I can't tell you, but it is enough to see me through the summer.'

What was her relationship with money?

'If you need more, earn more.'

Churchill's personal finances were always a worry to his wife and each personal financial crisis was inevitably sorted out by writing more books and paying less tax. An excellent book on Churchill, by Peter Clarke, published in 2012, details all of this in a very readable way. Clarke looked at Churchill's personal finances, by reviewing his correspondence, his bank account, his tax returns and even his unsurprisingly huge wine bills ('about three times the earnings of a male manual worker at the time').

Few of us are in the position where the next book deal or false eyelash promotion is easy to come by, but we can all give the concept of earning more money sensible consideration. Also, a second job is not just about earning more money, it can also be the route to spending less. If you work in a pub on a Saturday night you are earning, not spending, and you are delivering yourself a social life at the same time. The same can be said of anyone working in a café or a bookshop, part-time.

There are three main ways to apply yourself to increasing your income:

- earning more from your current job
- taking a second job, and
- sweating your assets.

This chapter will look at all of them, and then it is for you to decide which will work for you.

It may be all of them!

# Earning more from your current job

There are three reasons why you may not be earning enough in your current job.

- You haven't asked.
- You are not experienced or qualified enough to earn more money.
- Your employer can't afford to pay you more money.

Let's look at these in turn.

## *You haven't asked*

Women are notoriously bad at asking for pay rises. Our inclination to please, with a helping hand from self-doubt, has a lot to answer for. It accounts for much of why many women don't speak up when they think they should be better paid. Often, we feel pathetically grateful to be paid whatever we are currently getting, and assess the other rewards for our work (flexible working, interesting occupation, sense of achievement) as a reason not to ask for more pay.

But accepting the status quo is not going to advance your financial goals very far.

Maybe the time has come to be more assertive when it comes to your salary.

Think back to your last pay review. Did you just accept the pay rise you were given, regardless of whether you thought it should have been more? Or the last bonus – the same? Perhaps it is time to learn one of the greatest life skills – saying no.

Emma Beddington, a freelance writer based in Brussels, who has to price her work every day, stresses that it is important to be assertive and to be aware of your worth: 'I'm constantly underselling myself, doing jobs for tiny amounts of money that simply aren't financially viable.'

Learn that saying a polite no isn't rude, or career suicide – it's often essential for your financial and emotional well-being.

Of course we would all like to be paid more money for what we do – and we can't always have that – but what I am talking about here is a potential situation in which you are being underpaid and need to speak out about it.

What are you paid now? How much do you think it should be? Why?

Go out and do some research. Find people who are doing jobs like yours in similar firms (LinkedIn makes this a lot easier than it used to be, even for more obscure jobs) and contact them to ask for some guidance. Get in touch with a recruiter who specializes in whatever you do and ask them for guidance, too.

Gather the evidence and then present it to your employer. Ask for a meeting to discuss it in a non-threatening way. Then just explain what you want to earn, and why you think you should be paid that particular amount.

Practise what you are going to say beforehand – on friends or your partner. When business leaders or politicians know they are going to be engaged in challenging interactions with others (for instance, being interviewed on live TV), they almost always practise beforehand to make sure they come across as confident, not arrogant. That is what you need to do before any discussion about compensation.

Being brave and unafraid of saying no is important in any salary negotiation. Let's take a different scenario. If you apply for a role through an advertisement or a recruiter, and you are offered the role, but with a salary that you believe should be higher, what should you do?

Assuming it is a job that you want, it is worth persisting to see if the employer will offer you more money. Write or call the person who sent you the offer and explain that you would really like to accept, but that you had hoped for a higher salary and – crucially – specify the higher figure. Then it is up to the employer to be honest with you about whether they can offer your required salary, or anything near it.

## *You are not experienced or qualified enough to earn more money*

On the face of it, this looks like it has a very easy solution. Just go out there and get the right qualifications and experience. But, of course, it's never that easy, is it?

Lots of things prevent us from taking some practical steps towards advancing our career and earning more. Lack of self-confidence – which, as discussed, affects women so much more than men – is often to blame.

Depending on how old you are, it may be tempting

to think that it is 'too late' to go and study for a formal qualification, but don't be put off. Not only is it never too late, but it has never been easier, in these days of the internet, to access further formal qualifications. Even if you are working in a remote fishery in the Orkneys, you can still do an MBA at the Open University.

Are you stuck in a career that has a natural upper limit?

Women, who are generally more organized than men, excel at administrative roles, which is why there are so many more female secretaries and PAs than men. But there's only so much people will pay for administrative support. So how do you progress from being a secretary?

I would suggest two routes.

First of all, find something else with a vocational qualification that you can study for in your spare time. The first PA I hired in my own business, the Lovely Lucinda, now working elsewhere, has been training as a counsellor in her spare time and plans to move to the profession full-time once she has qualified and done the required amount of training hours.

Another way is to build up trust with someone who can give you that break into a non-secretarial job. Most people who are given the chance to try their hand at something different and potentially more lucrative are the beneficiaries of a great relationship with their boss – something they have earned through assiduous hard work and reliability in their original post. Whatever it is that you want to do, find the company that does it, then join as a secretary (even a temp, if necessary). Make sure you get to work for the most senior person possible, proving yourself, before asking for a transfer.

### *Your employer can't afford to pay you more money*

This may well be true. If you work in a small business, with narrow margins, it simply may not be possible for the company to pay you what you ought to be paid. But in that case, are the other benefits (flexibility and so on) worth the discount? If you have set your financial goals and know that the company just won't be able to help you achieve them, then you will have to leave and get a role somewhere bigger.

Pay rises, transfers to new jobs – these things don't happen overnight. You should not expect to achieve everything immediately. It's not a matter of saying that you want a pay rise, then threatening to leave if you don't get it. But you should signal clearly your desire for a second pay rise, or a transfer to a non-secretarial role, or whatever your goal is, and then set your own, private date by which, if it hasn't happened, you will think about your other options.

## Taking a second job

You may have found the perfect job for you at this time in your life but would still like to earn more money to meet your financial goals.

Zoe Free, aged twenty-four, from Telford, has a very rewarding day job, working for a charity that provides residential homes for children who have suffered trauma or neglect. But with a salary of just £20,000, and a financial goal to buy a flat, she needed to earn more income. Zoe qualified as a Zumba instructor and worked evenings and weekends, earning an additional £100 to £125 a week. 'Without it,' she said, 'I would struggle for the small things in life, like going out with friends. It's a real lifesaver.'

After I was married and had Cost Centre #1, I decided to do an MBA and my employer let me work part-time to attend classes, not all of which were in the evenings. (Yes, I know. Newly married, small baby, and do an MBA? I was young and clearly thought I didn't need much sleep.) But while I didn't want to leave that job (I knew that continuity was essential to the health of my future CV) neither could we cope financially without my original salary. So I got a second job too, writing articles for anyone and everyone, on whatever subject they wanted. This was something I could do in the evenings, when the baby had gone to sleep and my essays were done.

So how about it then? A second job in your spare time?

Before telling yourself that you don't have the time, bear in mind that the average woman spends fifty-nine days in her lifetime on that most hated of all beauty chores: shaving her legs.

The second-job routine is not limited to Zoe and me.

No fewer than one in ten police officers in the UK have second jobs. These include being a vicar, a pole dancing teacher, pallbearer, undertaker, ski instructor, ice-cream salesman and a medium. Others offer training in self-defence or firing taser guns.

## *How will you find a second job?*

Try the direct approach, starting with the places local to you. Where do you occasionally hang out? Or eat? People like employing locals and people who are known to them.

Look online or in the local phone book to see where your nearest contract catering company is. They may want help at the weekends (for weddings and so forth).

Get a qualification that will allow you to do a second job, like Zoe and her Zumba instructing. My safety pilot, Wonderful Wayne, has an HGV licence. When he needed a second job, he drove lorries at night – jobs that he got through a local agency. Getting an HGV licence may be a great investment!

You could go online to see what part-time or week-end jobs are available, or even if there are any jobs that you can do from home. Check out the freelance website www.peopleperhour.com. At the time of writing there are almost 200 writing jobs on there which, if I was still in need of additional writing income, I could bid for.

Remember this, though: check that taking a second job doesn't breach the terms of your current employment contract, and that you are paying the correct amount of tax. If you are receiving maternity pay from your employer, or statutory maternity pay, you are not allowed to work.

### *Working lots of jobs at the same time – going freelance*

Like me, lots of people choose flexibility over money and then find that they have to supplement their income. Giving up your job and going freelance, and then getting as much work as possible, can give you more flexibility while keeping your income at about the same level.

It can also often be more tax efficient, allowing you to hold on to more of your cash. A freelance writer, for instance, will be able to claim travel expenses as well as computer expenses against tax. And anyone working from home will be able to claim a proportion of their home expenses (utility bills and similar) against tax.

But working freelance is tough.

## Emma and her jobs

Emma Beddington is thirty-eight, British, and has been based in Brussels for the past six years with her long-term partner and two children, aged nine and ten.

She is a former lawyer now turned restaurant critic for the Eurostar magazine *Metropolitan*. She writes travel guides and features for other travel magazines, and does ad hoc features work for women's magazines such as *Red* and *Elle*. She has also worked quite regularly for the *Guardian* 'Family' section in the last couple of years. She additionally still does legal consultancy work on a retainer basis for a legal publishing company.

Does she think that going freelance works financially?

'The financial uncertainty is compensated by the feeling that at least I'm giving it a shot – if I hadn't tried to make my living as a writer at some point, I think I'd have regretted it bitterly. I've also learned a great deal about what I'm good at and what I'm terribly bad at, and in a way, it's taken away some of my "if only" thoughts. Knowing what I do now, I don't think I'd have been a good journalist earlier in my life, so I have less envy and frustration when I look at the careers of others.

'The fear, though, is hard. There is no security, no sense that financially I will be okay. I've completely lost that cosy insouciance. Every bill is a calculation and often a struggle. I know I'm okay for my next tax bill, but I have nightmares about the one after that.

'I do all sorts of work to supplement my income – translation, editing and, yes, legal consultancy. Without that law job, I would have gone under over the past year, when several of the magazines I worked for regularly folded, and work was scarce.'

## *Hosting a home selling party*

If getting a second job working locally is proving impossible, you could work from home as a sales agent for a company. This may sound horrendous, but it can be quite fun – and, more to the point, it can get you those things you want to buy but can't afford.

By hosting your own home selling party you can earn anything from 25 per cent commission upwards. There's usually a small start-up cost, but the main thing you need is a bit of time, enthusiasm and commitment, and some living-room space. There is a huge variety of products to sell, and different companies offer different experiences. To host a party that suits you, go to www.findaparty.co.uk.

Some people take to this with great success.

Julie Knight was a teacher who decided to work part-time 'to see my children grow up' and then needed a second job to meet the growing costs of her family. She took up home selling with Kleeneze in 2009. Julie has been so successful that what started as her second job (two days a week, fitted around part-time teaching) has now become her main income. And she only teaches two days a week now.

Before you put this book down and think you could never do anything of the sort, let me tell you that I did this myself. And it was really worth it.

Last year, I received an email from Johnnie Boden, the owner of the eponymous company whose clothes have been adorning the bodies of the UK's yummy mummies (and their children and husbands and friends and, indeed, everyone they know) for more than twenty years. It has now expanded to the USA, France, Germany and Austria.

I am used to receiving emails from Mr Boden, because I am a willing recipient of his catalogues – although the purchases I occasionally make are rarely for me. But this email was not trying to sell me clothes. The heading said: 'Do you fancy holding a Boden shopping party?'

It went on to explain that this was effectively a pop-up Boden shop, held for one day in my home. 'Think Tupperware with rails of lovely clothes,' Mr Boden's email continued. 'If you are intrigued, please contact . . .'

The first thing you have to do, it turns out, is pass the Boden test on location selection.

'The last thing that we want,' said the next email that I received (after confirming that I was, indeed, 'intrigued'), 'is something resembling a jumble sale.'

Indeed not! (Although it has to be said that, when all the Cost Centres are home, a jumble sale would be an upmarket description.)

Boden wanted the occasion to be 'a great experience' and 'lots of fun' for those attending. No pressure then. I would also need lots of mirrors (not something I have a great many of, considering that I have a BMI of 37).

I had to have a telephone interview with Boden to confirm the suitability of my home, which took almost a month to set up thanks to Davos, US book tours and so on. I must have passed, because I was then granted a date: 13 April 2013.

I opened my home to anyone in or near South Oxfordshire wanting to see/touch/try Boden clothes – or, indeed, just find out what my house looks like – from 10 a.m. to 4 p.m. I invited all my friends, sent a note round the village, and allowed Boden to alert their local customers. To ensure the 'lots of fun' part, I rented a bouncy castle.

Boden sent me three key things prior to the event. The first was a £50 voucher to buy something from the spring/summer range, which, as the weather had been anything but spring/summer recently, I raffled off in aid of the church bell restoration fund. The second was some freshly brewed coffee. I am not a fan of coffee, but I can take a hint. So I went and found my cafetière and gave it a good wash. The final thing was a scented candle (presumably in case my house smelled bad).

I was also sent a laminated card with five final tips, including decluttering my home 'as if it were up for sale'. I duly decluttered, banished Mr M to the golf course, outsourced the two dogs, sent Cost Centres #1 and #3 away, and put #2 in charge of the car parking (on the local recreation ground).

Guests who placed orders at my party got 20 per cent off plus free delivery. I got quite a lot of things out of the party: the opportunity to meet several neighbours I had not previously been acquainted with; the chance to invite some friends over (including many we had not seen for ages); and about £700 in commission. Even better, I exchanged my commission for Boden vouchers, which meant they gave me 50 per cent more – so a total of £1,050. All the Cost Centres will be dressed in Boden for some time.

## Sweat your assets

If you own your house, that will be your biggest asset. So why not use it to pay for its keep?

### *Rent out a room*

If you have a spare room in your house, why not rent it out? The government's rent-a-room scheme lets you earn rent tax free on a furnished room, or entire floor, for up to £4,250 per year (though this is halved if you share the income with someone else). Per week this means you can charge £81.70 before you start paying tax on it. All you have to remember is to let your insurance provider – and landlord (if applicable) – know that you are taking in a lodger. If you live alone, it may also affect your single person's council tax discount, so do check with your local authority.

You can pay to advertise your room on websites such as crashpadder.com (now part of Airbnb) or www.mondaytofriday.com.

Or advertise for free on www.spareroom.co.uk. And if you live near a university or college, it's a good idea to get in touch with their housing department.

You could also register with Airbnb (www.airbnb.co.uk) for out-of-towners needing a room for a shorter period. You can choose whether to be there when they stay, and it's a great way to meet people from all around the world. They've mostly been vetted by previous hosts, too, so you don't have to panic about them taking the family silver. At a *Guardian* newspaper event on sustainable business in November 2012, the co-founder of Airbnb related the touching story of a woman who couldn't travel for health reasons. To make sure her son didn't miss out on seeing the world, she advertised a room so that her guests might explain what life was like back in their home country.

If you live in a big city, renting out your home while you are on holiday will probably help pay for your holiday – see www.holidaylettings.co.uk.

You can also register your home for free with Sarah Eastel Locations (www.film-locations.co.uk). A typical home could earn anything from £750 to £5,000 per twelve hours for a feature film. Music videos can net you between £500 and £3,000, and documentaries between £400 and £1,000 a day. Other websites you may want to try are www.locationworks.com and www.shootfactory.co.uk. Do check beforehand what their charges will be, however.

## *Rent out your driveway*

If you don't want strangers invading your home, you could rent out your driveway instead. You will need to sign a contract stating that you are not responsible for the parked vehicle, but most websites will provide that information when you sign up. Have a look at www.yourparkingspace.co.uk and www.parkatmyhouse.com. According to these websites, this can earn you £90 a week in London, for example, or £35 in York.

## *Rent out your car*

In some cities in the USA you can even rent out your car via www.getaround.com – and how much do you really use your car? Anyone who is nineteen, or older, with a 'good' driving record can sign up, and international licences are accepted. You can rent out your car by the hour or by the day, there are no membership fees, and Getaround provides full insurance cover together with 24/7 roadside assistance. Hopefully, this will come to the UK before too long.

## *Rent out your storage space*

If you've got spare storage space in your home, whether it is a loft, garage or room, there's money to be made if you rent it out. To find potential customers, visit the websites www.storemates.co.uk and www.spareground.co.uk and www.storenextdoor.com to post a listing.

These websites offer guidelines and rules to ensure a safe and legitimate exchange, so be sure to read them carefully before committing. And before leasing your space, always check whether doing so would invalidate your insurance policy.

### *Rent out equipment*

You can also earn money from renting out your tools, sports equipment, furniture or skills through websites such as ecomodo.com and www.rentmyitems.com.

## Make sure your savings are earning as much interest as they should be

What interest are you getting on your ISA or your savings account?

Even though ISAs are tax free, they often have very low rates. Shop around to make sure you are getting the best rate.

If you have cash in the bank that you don't think you will need for a while, ask your bank how much interest you would get on it if you deposited it for a fixed period of time. Banks like to know that they can rely on your cash being there, so the longer you are prepared to lend it to them, the more they will pay for the privilege.

Earning more is unlikely to be the answer to all your financial problems, but it probably would help. (Don't think, however, that you can ignore all the other chapters in this book if you get a second job, or manage to increase your income in some way. But it is a good start in the right direction.)

I have had many jobs over the years, and rarely only one at a time. It takes creativity, education and sacrifice and, even while I am writing this, there are so many other things I could have done. But I have committed to a second career as a writer, and so this takes priority.

Like everything else discussed in this book, it takes time and focus to achieve what you want.

But it is worth it.

## Earning more

- Make sure you are well prepared for your next pay review. Do the research, and have a specific figure in mind that you would like to be paid.
- Should you be considering a course or qualification to enable you to earn more? Ask your employer what you could do to improve your earning potential.
- Is there a second job you could be doing at the weekend, which would also help your social life? Write down all the places you go to. See if you could get a job working at any of them.
- Is there something you could do at home to help you earn more? Rent out a room? Become a representative for a jewellery or make-up company? If you are a social person with a lot of friends, holding jewellery or make-up parties may suit you very well. Or how about Ann Summers?!

## CHAPTER 7

# BEING YOUR OWN BOSS

When I was twenty-three, back in 1985, I was contacted by two women who had founded an executive search company which, in those days, handled appointments in advertising and public relations. They wanted to suggest me as a candidate for a position they were filling for a client.

Airdre Taylor and Annita Bennett had met each other while working for the advertising agency Lintas, in 1981, and resolved to set up their own company. They went to look at buying existing businesses (an upholstery workshop round the back of King's Cross being one of them) and decided to start their own instead.

Their company was set up with the aim of finding people for jobs and saving employers the headache of running advertisements and sifting through the replies. They put in a small amount of money each, rented a cheap walk-up office on the third floor of a building near Chancery Lane tube station, and opened for business. Lintas gave them their first assignment.

During the subsequent twenty-two years, they grew the company to invoicing £1.5 million a year, never borrowed any money and funded the whole of their expansion from cash flow.

I still have all the original handwritten accounts from the start of this business. Why? Because, in 2004, twenty-two years after it had been founded, I bought it.

When I was headhunted by those women, back in 1985, I went forward as a candidate for the role and got it, starting as an advertising planner with BMP (now Adam & Eve DDB). But what really impressed me was the professionalism of the company that had contacted me. I was fascinated by their business model and stayed in touch with them over the years. And I vowed to try to buy the company, if the opportunity ever arose.

Time moved on and I did an MBA, swapping the world of advertising and PR for the world of banking. In 2000, when I sensed my fascination with banking was drawing to a close, I contacted Airdre and Annita, who were still running the business, and persuaded them to hire me and teach me to be a headhunter.

In 2002, when one partner retired, I bought 20 per cent of the business from her. In 2004, I bought the rest of it, paying for it with a mixture of loan notes – essentially IOUs made out to the vendors – and bank debt. In total I paid £1.8 million for the company and, apart from rolling over the 20 per cent I already had, I borrowed every penny. A small part of the borrowing (£250,000) was secured by my Other Single Girlfriend with a mortgage on her house, something she was released from less than three years later.

## Women and entrepreneurialism

Working for yourself may be the fastest way to get to your financial finish line. A study published in January 2013 showed that affluent, established female business owners in the UK are earning an average of 14 per cent a year more than their male counterparts. Women, it argued, 'may be better rewarded in a more entrepreneurial environment'.

In the USA, as of 2012, it is estimated that there are over 8.3 million businesses owned by women, generating nearly $1.3 trillion in revenue. And women are founding businesses at 1.5 times the national average.

Worldwide, thousands of women are setting up businesses that create jobs and deliver wider social and environmental benefits. Many of today's most successful ethical brands had visionary women at their roots: The Body Shop, Green and Black's, People Tree. Another attraction of social enterprise for women, in particular, is its focus on long-term impacts, as opposed to short-term gains. Statistics show that women in business take fewer risks, favouring stability over profit potential.

## What may hold you back?

Women suffer disproportionately from a lack of self-confidence. And if you ever needed self-confidence, it is when starting or buying a business!

According to the UK government, men tend to have more positive entrepreneurial attitudes than women, mainly due to the difference in their self-perception of the skills they possess. Only 29 per cent of non-entrepreneurially active women agreed with the statement 'I have the skills, knowledge and experience to start a business' compared with 45 per cent of men. Even many of those who agreed that good start-up options were available said they would not pursue them, for fear of failure.

## *Believe in yourself*

Brynne Kennedy Herbert, the UK-based founder and CEO of global employee relocation company MOVE Guides, has observed that entrepreneurship requires determination and vision, and 'immense personal belief'. When starting her business – essentially a tech company – she faced a big gap between vision and execution, involving 'challenging organizational logistics that no one tells you about'.

Renée Elliott, also an American living in London, was thirty when she set up Planet Organic.

'I thought that I was young enough to start over again, if it didn't work out. At the time I was surrounded by British naysayers who were worried it might not work, in contrast to my American friends who were like "you go, girl". It makes sense to surround yourself with friends who are supportive.'

Renée says that, at nineteen, she was very shy but passionate and determined. And she believed in her ability to sell. She acknowledges that self-confidence is key.

> As a "nobody" without private education and money behind you, you might think it is easier for those of privilege. But as Baron Joffe once said to me, "knowing how to lead" is the most important thing in life.

Energy meter inventor Tanya Ewing says that she never worried about whether she would be able to raise the finance to support her company: 'I felt it was obvious it was going to be a success.'

### *Being risk-aware is good – and so is listening*

When it comes to entrepreneurship, women may be more risk-aware than men. Understanding the risks that face a business, and knowing how you will deal with any challenges that arise, is critical. Women are also more likely to listen and take advice than men.

These combined factors may explain why women can make such great entrepreneurs.

As Sylvia Ann Hewlett, President and CEO of the Center for Talent Innovation, argues: 'If you have the power of different kinds of perspectives and backgrounds, you will create better decisions, discover opportunities to hit new markets, and create new products.'

Juliet Davenport of Good Energy is a good example. In 2003, her company was the first to offer electricity from 100 per cent renewable sources to UK households.

She pops in for a cup of tea and a chat with her customer care team on a regular basis, drawing on their experiences to find out what will persuade more consumers to buy her wares. Her willingness to listen and her appetite for innovation may seem unrelated – but they're not.

## How to go about getting your business funded

But even if you have a great idea, how are you going to get it funded?

Read on, to find out the main ways to go about turning your business idea into a reality.

Before you even start looking for the money, you need to make sure you have both the passion for the project – to enable you to withstand the tough times – and a highly detailed business plan. Both these things will help you to convince prospective funders that you are a good prospect.

### *You need a passion for what you want to do*

Chantal Coady started Rococo Chocolates thirty years ago, armed with a degree in textile design and a passion for chocolate, plus a belief that there was nowhere in the UK where you could buy high-quality product. She took herself off to work in the chocolate department of a high-end department store to learn something about it, and then went on a short business course before going to the bank manager with her business plan.

Nowadays, Chantal is one of the best chocolate chefs around and has written several books on the subject. But back in 1983, she didn't know how to make chocolate. So she sold products from small chocolate makers and sugared almonds found at a trade show in Cologne. But within a decade, Rococo would be producing its own chocolates – originally made in the kitchen at Chantal's home – and the company has never looked back.

Renée Elliott believes that to start a business you need passion and clarity. 'Your passion is the focus of your business, as well as your team and your customers,' she says.

Brynne Kennedy Herbert has a passion for her business, and also took advantage of what she saw as a massive gap in the market.

In the 1990s, when I moved around the world – from London to Hong Kong to Singapore and then to Tokyo – either my employer or my husband's engaged a relocation agent who would help us find a house, open a bank account and get our children into a suitable school, plus arrange to ship our goods to the next destination.

In the twenty-first century so many people are being moved around the world by their employers (or hired from overseas) that expensive relocation agents are no longer possible for any but the most senior people. Brynne's idea was to design a web and mobile platform that would make it easy for companies to move employees on a budget – and therefore help companies get the right talent in the right place.

## *Do lots of research and then prepare a detailed business plan*

You will need a detailed business plan to show your prospective funders – whether they are your mum, the bank manager or a group of professional investors. There are many books and online tutorials about how to write a business plan, so I won't repeat the details here.

Useful websites include http://www.startupdonut.co.uk/startup/business-planning/writing-a-business-plan.

If you are under thirty, living in England and Wales (or under twenty-five in Scotland), check out http://www.princes-trust.org.uk/need-help/enterprise-programme/explore-where-to-start/business-plans/business-plan-templates.aspx.

There is plenty of help available when you come to write a business plan, and there are many government and not-for-profit initiatives to advise you. The Prince's Trust can assign you a mentor, for example.

Renée Elliott, the aforementioned founder of Planet Organic, left her job as a professional wine writer and found help at her local unemployment office. She was offered a course on how to set up a business, which she found 'invaluable'. She also learned on the job, as well as from her accountant and her husband (who has spent many years in commercial property). 'He was very interested in screwing the costs down and was quite nosey, but offered good advice.' See, being a good listener helps!

Remember, writing a business plan takes time.

Tanya Ewing, the founder and former CEO of Ewgeco, a company that makes real-time energy monitors, found herself unexpectedly grounded for a sad reason. But she used the time wisely to write her business plan. Having fallen pregnant with twins, she miscarried one of them, was ordered to rest and spent several days in hospital. 'I had been receiving so much information from so many sources, I wasn't sure what to do next,' she explains, 'so this quiet time really helped.'

The opportunity for quiet reflection also helped her to work out what was going to be important when it came to raising money: 'As the look of my invention was as important as the technology, I decided that instead of a prototype – normally quite ugly, cumbersome and expensive – I would create a mock-up of the user interface.'

Tanya did a lot of research before formulating that plan. You, too, will need to do a lot of research – even to the point of going to work in a competing or similar enterprise to get first-hand experience. As I mentioned, Rococo Chocolates founder Chantal Coady got herself a job working in the chocolate department of an upmarket department store in order to do just that.

MOVE Guides' Brynne Kennedy Herbert also went to work somewhere to get experience before finalizing her business plan – a couple of investment banks and then me. Brynne is a focused blonde whose excellent deportment betrays her earlier days in elite gymnastics. What betrays her extraordinary work ethic is that she continued to compete, with the Yale Bulldogs, while studying for her undergraduate degree at Yale.

In March 2011, I was a speaker at the Women in Business Conference staged by the female students of the London Business School, where Brynne was a student. I graduated with my MBA from LBS, way back in 1992, and this was not the first time I had spoken at the event. I gave a brief talk about career points for women, and then afterwards I ran a workshop teaching people how to network effectively. I encouraged the audience to decide on what they wanted to achieve, and who they wanted to meet, and to go after them purposefully.

So I can't have been surprised when I got an email from Brynne – who I didn't know, but who had been in the audience that day. She was looking for a mentor and wanted to learn from an established female entrepreneur. Would I be that person? Could she come and spend time with me at work, to shadow me?

Now, like everyone else, I only have 168 hours in the week, and I get requests like this all the time. So the answer was no. But the email was well written and phrased in the right way. It was to the point, but not overly pushy, and clearly demonstrated her ambition and potential. So when, three months later, I decided that I needed some temporary help, I emailed her and asked if she was available to work for me for the summer while building MOVE Guides.

She worked for me for three months, and here is the irony in the tale – I have ended up learning so much more about how to be a female entrepreneur from her than she would ever have learned if I had acceded to her original request to shadow me for a day or two at work.

## *However you raise the money, cash is king*

The cash flow statement is the most important document in the whole of your business plan. It shows – ideally, week by week – how much cash you will need and for what. Prepare that, and then imagine that you won't sell anything for a while.

How long can you continue in business? How much cash do you need?

If your business idea involves selling to customers who pay immediately – whether by cash or near-cash (for example, credit cards) – you may not need much cash. Chantal's original company would have needed cash to rent and fit out her shop, but she could potentially have bought the inventory on credit from suppliers and sold it for cash, which is how most retailers operate.

However, when you are a completely new business,

most suppliers will be reluctant to sell to you for anything except cash. Lacking a track record always makes it harder to do anything.

So, before you go and get your business funded, you have to know just how much cash you are going to need. And, just as importantly, how quickly you will be able to pay it back.

The more you need, and the longer it will be before you will see any return, the more likely you are to need equity investors (i.e. people who will own the company alongside you).

Brynne needed to spend hundreds of thousands of pounds on hiring people to write computer code to make her mobile app and website. She knew she wouldn't make a profit for a while, so she went out and raised the money from equity investors.

Jack Dorsey, the CEO of Twitter, sent out his famous first tweet in 2006. Twitter raised no fewer than eight rounds of finance from equity investors before it listed on the stock exchange, in 2013, and it still was not profitable.

Facebook was founded in 2004, and did not make a profit until 2008.

These types of companies, where getting your business running requires lots of upfront investment, are always much better funded by people who are prepared to wait a long time for the return.

If you need a sizeable amount of cash to get started but will be bringing some in pretty quickly – as with Chantal's chocolates – or if (like me) you are buying an existing business with proven cash flow, then a bank loan may be the best route. However, if you don't need very much – your business idea involves doing something without large overheads (like my godson, who started his business career selling cricket bats on eBay) – you may be able to find it from your own resources, as the founders of my business did in 1982.

## The principal ways to fund a business

We have seen three ways to fund a business:

- using equity investors (like Brynne)
- self-investing and growing through cash flow (like Airdre Taylor and Annita Bennett), and
- borrowing money (like me).

Which is best for you?

If you have read the rest of the book, you will already know that I can't answer every question, and this is one of them. You, and you alone, will know what is best for you, because you alone will know how much cash you will need and how quickly cash will start coming in.

But while I can't tell you which way is best for you, I can show you how they all work.

So read on to find out about the main ways to fund a business. And then – probably even more importantly – read my tips on how to make sure you put yourself in the best possible position to raise the finance for your business successfully, whichever financing route you choose.

## *Bank financing*

Borrowing money from the bank is just as time-consuming as raising equity capital.

Women are better at getting bank loans than men, because they are better at putting more detail into their loan applications.

According to a study of more than 20,000 businesses, conducted on behalf of the UK government in mid-2013, about 70 per cent of loan applications from SMEs led by women secured a loan, compared with 56 per cent of their male counterparts. The two main reasons for this were that women were more likely to have a detailed business plan and also to have someone with a financial qualification in charge of the finances. (See my later comment on credibility.)

Banks will impose strict conditions on companies who borrow money. You may want to take a tip from how very successful companies, with strong cash flow, borrow money. They work out what they need to borrow, then write to a number of banks and ask them if they would be interested in lending it to them. What they are trying to find out from each bank is (a) how much interest the bank will charge, (b) how often the bank wants repayments to be made and (c) what covenants (i.e. what specific conditions) the bank will insist on. Those are the main terms for any bank loan. They are all things that you, too, should find out – and compare, if you are lucky enough to have more than one offer.

### What is a covenant?

For many companies (mine included) the covenants are the critical part.

Imagine that, when you borrowed the money for your mortgage, the bank said that they would only lend you the money for as long as your income remained above a certain amount. This means that, if you lost your job at any time, and had no income for a while, the bank would immediately repossess the house, even if you had been making the repayments regularly while unemployed and managed to get another job very quickly.

Covenants are like that. They may insist on a certain level of profitability, or a specific level of sales, or state that some ratio or other (for example, staff costs to sales) has to be at a certain level. Some companies, when writing to banks asking them to bid for their business, state which covenants they will, or will not, agree to.

Asking banks to bid for your business – and, indeed, saying what you will or won't agree to by way of conditions – is for well-established companies who are household names with excellent credit ratings and strong cash flow. You, on the other hand, will almost certainly have none of those things just yet. But it is a good exercise to consider whether you will accept the conditions (i.e. the covenants) the bank will place on you.

## Should you offer a personal guarantee?

This is something banks usually insist on as a condition of lending, especially to new businesses. It means that, if the business fails and can't repay the money, you will be liable to pay it back personally.

I would encourage you, if at all possible, not to offer a personal guarantee.

I have had to offer these from time to time – and I currently personally guarantee one quarter of my company's borrowings – but every time I borrow money for any of my business interests I try very hard indeed not to do it. Whether you will manage to get out of doing this depends on how much the bank wants your business. Sometimes you have no choice.

When Tanya Ewing's company was promised seed funding of £100,000 by Scottish Enterprise, they were counting on the money. But then the quango changed its mind, citing the very early stage of development. 'We had to sign the house over to get the funds. It was the only option,' she admits.

## Should you secure the loan?

A loan can be secured to your property or other assets. Or you may ask someone else to do so.

When Chantal Coady borrowed her bank loan to start Rococo Chocolates, her mother secured the loan for her. If you do this – or someone does it for you – and the company fails, you may have to sell your home.

We sold our home and moved into rented accommodation *before* I bought my business in 2004, which meant that we didn't have any property to offer security on. My Other Single Girlfriend came to my rescue and guaranteed the last £250,000 of my borrowing by securing it to her flat. That was a heroic thing to do, and was a great act of faith in me.

My choice regarding finding the last £250,000 was this: either I get the money from an equity investor, in which case (at the time) I would have had to give away 16 per cent of the business, or I give OSG a much smaller part of the business (around 5 per cent) for offering the guarantee. It was a no-brainer, in my opinion.

You may be lucky enough to have a wonderful friend, as I did. Or, like Chantal Coady, you may have a wonderful mother. But getting other people to secure your business loan is a big ask. There are real risks associated with this, and it is not to be undertaken lightly.

### Are there any good government schemes to help me borrow money?

I have borrowed money for my business under the Enterprise Finance Guarantee, whereby I pay a fee to the government for guaranteeing three-quarters of the company's debt.

Not every bank offers the EFG, but it is worth looking into if you already have an established, viable business and need a guarantee. You can find out more at https://www.gov.uk/understanding-the-enterprise-finance-guarantee.

## *Banks are not the only places that lend money*

You can borrow from friends and family, of course, and from the people you are buying from (as I did), but there are other organizations that will lend to people starting a business.

- *Specialist companies set up for the purpose.* These are often backed, directly or indirectly, by the government. By September 2013, the company Start Up Loans (www.startuploans.co.uk) had lent more than £45.5 million and backed more than 7,839 businesses. They also offer mentoring and support.
- *Crowdfunding (peer-to-peer lending or equity investment).* This is an area where women in business are really excelling, according to Erika Watson, Editor of Prowess 2.0, the online centre for women in business. It brings together micro-investments and social media. This works well for women, given their online communication style. The Funding Circle (www.fundingcircle.com) has grown rapidly since being founded. Zopa is another peer-to-peer lending service (www.zopa.com), which has 42,000 active lenders and has loaned £363 million since it was set up in 2005.
- *Not-for-profit organizations.* If you don't need much money, there are also not-for-profit organizations such as Social Baank (www.socialbaank.com) – and no, those are not typos, the two 'a's denote that it is

not a traditional bank – which will lend up to £1,000 to new borrowers and not require any security. Community Development Finance Institutions (CDFIs) are not-for-profit finance providers that provide small loans alongside support and financial advice. This kind of package particularly appeals to a lot of female-led start-ups, because women are more likely to value the support and training.

- *Credit cards.* Plenty of people (for example, the founders of Innocent smoothies) start businesses on credit cards. It is not strictly what they are for, but you can get some good rates – even zero per cent in some cases – and if you don't need much money, it may be a very sensible route.

## *Equity investors*

Women find equity investors hard to access, according to Erika Watson. She doesn't suggest why, but I believe I know.

Women are much less likely to have invested in social capital – relationships – than men, focusing instead on doing a good job at work and then rushing home to make sure the family are cared for. And yet, the very first place to look for equity investors is among the people you already know.

If it is scary borrowing money from a bank, it is doubly scary taking money from friends and family because you will feel the risk of losing it so much more keenly. But they will be the best place to start.

Renée Elliott of Planet Organic didn't have very much money of her own to help start her company. One of her earliest investors was her best friend, who had inherited money from her grandfather. 'When she offered it, I said, "Really? Oh, please don't. It's a huge risk. Please only put half in." But she put it all in. It really freaked me out!'

Renée had originally set up the business with someone she had met when working in a health-food store. His family and friends were also early private investors. Planet Organic is a strongly value-led business, and Renée stresses that it is important that investors in a company like hers buy into the concept right from the start: 'Otherwise, you'll waste time defending what you're doing. You all need to be on the same page.' Renée also accepted equity investors who offered their services as payment for shares, such as her architect.

Tanya Ewing was raising her first round of funding during the financial crisis and remembers how tough it was to get investors on board. She raised £700,000 through a syndicate of friends, family and neighbours, alongside a public company and a pension fund. Her investor drive included a cocktail party to launch her prototype, to which she invited utility companies, banks, IP people and 'anyone I thought might invest in Ewgeco'.

## What about crowdfunding?

Take a look at crowdfunding equity websites, such as Crowdcube (www.crowdcube.com) and Seedrs (www.seedrs.com).

Kinopto, a cinema server solution, raised £35,000 from twenty-one investors for 15 per cent equity, in seven days, through Crowdcube, to launch their product to market.

Gem Misa, founder of Righteous salad dressings, raised £75,000 from eighty-two investors for 15 per cent equity, in just over a month, also through Crowdcube, to fund future growth.

## *Funding your business from cash flow*

If your business plan does not show cash arriving immediately – and let's face it, that is very unlikely – then if you want to avoid both debt *and* equity investors, you may have to find another way of bringing in the cash to help the business grow. And even if you are going to borrow money or invite equity investors into your business, you are more likely to be able to do so if the business is already a little way along the road. This is why lots of entrepreneurs keep the day job going while starting their company.

Brynne worked for me for three months and used all the money she earned to pay developers who were writing code for her business idea. She did this because she wanted to have something to show equity investors when she went out to raise money.

When Tanya Ewing was setting up her business, she did other people's ironing to cover her travel costs when meeting the advisers, lawyers, organizations and other clever people from whom she had been receiving free advice and help. She didn't even own a laptop, and had to rely on lots of scribbled notes plus 'a Dictaphone that had set me back £70 – at the time, laptops were about £800, which was beyond my ironing capability'.

But to get the company further along before offering investors some of it, she asked her husband to sell his flat, which they had kept as an investment property after buying the marital home. 'We got £50,000 profit from this, giving the new business a really good start,' she said. It also – critically – showed potential investors that she was prepared to take some of the risk.

Renée Elliott's husband kept working to support her while she set up Planet Organic, although he did eventually quit and become her managing director.

### Cash from the business itself is ideal, but may slow your growth

Once you start making money, you can fund growth from the profits of the company itself.

The founders of my company never borrowed any money and only hired more people, or invested further in the business, as and when they had enough cash in the bank to do so.

This is very prudent, and to be admired, but it will slow your progress.

That may be fine, as it was for my founders. Between starting up the company in 1982 and selling it to me in

2004, a period of twenty-two years, they had grown it from £0 in revenue to £1.5 million; it took me only four more years, with borrowed money, to increase the revenue by another £1.5 million.

On the other hand, if (like Tanya) you know that others may try to imitate your idea, and you need to be first to market, it may not be the best way.

## What else do I need to know about how to finance my business successfully?

Now that you know the main ways to raise money, and can put some thought into which – if any of them – you want to explore, here are some strong tips for making sure that your business is appropriately funded and supported through its early stages.

### *Make sure you submit entries for competitions and awards*

Okay, you are probably very busy, and the last thing you have time for is writing a competition entry, plus you may be rather worried that, by exposing your idea, you will give secrets away to the competition.

But competitions/awards are useful for four reasons.

## The prize is often money and/or business advice to help you

Darrah Brustein is barely thirty and is an entrepreneur in Georgia, USA. When only twenty-five, three years after leaving university, she founded a publishing business that produces financial education books for children, *Finance Whiz Kids*.

'As a grown-up, I realized there were few, if any, resources for children of elementary age. And research shows that children start learning about money at age three. I wanted to create a series that would be informative but would not make parents feel that they were inadequate, or that it was a bad topic to discuss. That was age appropriate, and with relatable characters.'

Darrah decided that she didn't want to give up control to outside investors, and entered the Pepsi Refresh competition – a marketing initiative whereby Pepsi gave millions of dollars of grants to promising business ideas with worthy aims. She came in the top 100, a highly commendable result among thousands of entrants – not least because the result depended largely on a public vote.

One of Tanya Ewing's key funding strategies in the early years of her business was to enter for as many awards as possible. She received £1,000 from Scottish Enterprise at the end of 2006. And in early 2007, she won the Female Scottish Innovation Award, which came with a year's worth of free legal advice. Having a baby in the middle of this did not deter her – although the latter award was presented twelve days after she gave birth, and she couldn't sit down because she had forgotten her ring cushion to relieve the pressure on her piles!

### Winning can impress potential funders

Even more importantly than providing direct funding, winning a competition or an award shows other potential funders that, in the eyes of recognized third parties, you are on to something. In 2008, Tanya Ewing won Inventor of the Year at the tenth annual British Female Inventor and Innovator of the Year Awards, which, she says, 'gave me a lot of credibility'.

### Awards are good opportunities for free publicity

This is very useful if you are trying to sell a product or service to as wide a public as possible. Kathryn Parsons, the talented young founder of Decoded, has won so many awards that I have almost lost count. But when news of each one reaches the media, it inspires another group of people to sign up to learn to code.

### They are a great boost for you and your team

You are all probably working very hard for relatively little reward, especially in the early days.

In 2013, Brynne Kennedy Herbert was awarded the Global Mobility Rising Star of the Year Award at the Americas Expatriate Management and Mobility Awards (the EMMAs). This followed a similar accolade in

Singapore, where she won the APAC Rising Star Award, along with the company's runner-up award for Most Innovative Use of Technology. For Brynne and her team, it was inspiring to know that they had been recognized by their peers in the relocation industry.

## *Make cash preservation your prime focus*

Ask any entrepreneur and they will tell you that they will do anything, and everything, to preserve cash – especially at the beginning.

Even when you get more cash, you should continue to treat it as a precious resource.

Tanya Ewing's company now sells to all sixteen top house-building companies in the UK, but she remembers vividly how tight money used to be in the business before they raised the £50,000 from the sale of her husband's flat. Even when they did have more money, their attitude did not change; when negotiating with a company, she would always be sure to squeeze something extra out of them. 'If I bought something, I would bargain for something additional or a reduced price.'

The last of the £50,000 was used to launch a prototype of her energy meter, in May 2007. For the event they bought M&S food (Tanya says 'it looked fancier than it was on ready-made platters') and she asked a friend to waitress for the day, as a favour.

She didn't pay herself a salary for the first four years: 'I wanted to pay others – they were pivotal in the business.' And she sought out cost-efficient labour (such as having a student on a business placement for a year, from Robert Gordon University).

She also made sure that she was never caught out by hidden costs, and always had contingency funds. 'There were some horrible decisions that had to be made along the way – I cashed in life policies, dropped our patent outside of Europe, and made people redundant.'

Darrah Brustein makes a point of trying to enjoy a lifestyle that doesn't increase as her income increases, which gives her more flexibility to expand her business.

## *Make use of invoice financing*

At one point, my business was owed more than six months' income by clients who were deliberately dragging their heels to pay us.

If people are bad at paying you, invoice financing – whereby you sell the money people owe you to other people, and they then collect the money – is one way to get the cash in more quickly. Market Invoice (www.marketinvoice.com) is an online invoice auction service that has lent £60 million against invoices in two years.

Dessi Bell is twenty-nine and founded her clothing company Zaggora in 2011. She explained why she uses invoice financing: 'It's a convenient way to get money quickly. Sometimes you wait months to be paid.' In August 2013, Bell auctioned an invoice of about £50,000 to six buyers. The cash was in her account two days later. Over two months she will pay 1 per cent of the invoice value.

## *Build credibility*

Funders like investing in or lending money to people who are wholly credible. I have already explained why competitions and awards help this. But so does knowing your market inside out and back to front, and demonstrating that you have done your research (like Chantal Coady working in that chocolate department).

Another way to ensure credibility is to show funders/lenders that their money will be properly looked after and accounted for (i.e. that you have proper controls in place). The easiest way to do this is to have the very best accountancy person you can find on board. I am not a qualified accountant but I do have an MBA and a PhD in structured finance, and I also employ a brilliant and commercially minded accountant, Catherine Reid, at Grant Thornton in Leeds, as my outside adviser. All of that gives the bank comfort.

Renée Elliott agrees: 'Hire the best financial person you can.'

Other things that help credibility, as already discussed, include showing that you are prepared to risk your own money (as Tanya Ewing did), having a detailed and well-researched business plan, and having some well-respected investors already committed to your business.

Brynne raised her seed funding after graduating from

the London Business School in 2012, securing £400,000 from top European angels including Sherry Coutu, Tom Hulme, Dale Murray, Sean Parker and Kevin Eyres. In November 2013, she raised second-round funding of US$1.8 million with several of the same angels but, crucially, also two key institutional investors: Notion Capital and NEA.

Why did they participate?

Jos White, partner at Notion Capital, explained.

‘The service takes advantage of three of the biggest trends in the technology industry – cloud computing, mobile and internationalization – and meets the expectations of a new generation of employees. In this way, we believe they have what it takes to disrupt their industry and build a very big business.’

Patrick Chung, partner at NEA, commented.

‘It takes great people to build great companies, and relocation has always been one of the most challenging – and often frustrating – aspects of the hiring process. We are excited to work with Brynne and the team at MOVE Guides to build on the company's tremendous momentum and capture the global market opportunity for a next-generation relocation service.’

## *Grants may be available for you*

Women do better than men on the whole in accessing small grants, according to Erika Watson, because they tend to be a lot more detailed and thorough in their applications.

Tanya Ewing didn't pursue any grants when setting up her business, although she may well have been eligible, because 'they were too time-consuming'. She was keen to get her energy meter to market as fast as possible, before someone copied it.

---

I started this chapter by introducing you to Brynne Kennedy Herbert. Brynne started her company from scratch, as a result of a very frustrating move to London with her husband. When she complained to him about the hassles she had encountered, he asked her why she didn't do something about it. Four years later, the company has moved thousands of people across continents.

Makes it sound easy? It wasn't.

But the lesson is: if you find a market need, and are prepared to invest your sweat as equity, then the backing is there.

Renée Elliott deserves the last word on this.

' If you think about it, we're always selling ourselves: to get into university, get a job, get married. So raising finance should be approached in the same way. If you don't have the money, and you can't raise it, you'll never be successful.

When starting a business, it's important to take baby steps; not everything has to be done at once. I'm naturally very optimistic but at one point, when Planet Organic needed more capital and my investors said to me, "Where's the money going to come from," I quoted Maharishi and quipped, "From wherever it is now. There's money everywhere." ❜

There is money everywhere. Don't hide your light under a bushel, remember to do your homework, write a detailed business plan and make sure your cash flow forecast is as accurate as possible.

Good luck – I know you will succeed.

## HOMEWORK FOR INDEPENDENT WOMEN

### Preparing to be your own boss

- If you want to start your own business, or buy an existing one, the very first thing you need is a business plan.
  Look at the website https://www.gov.uk/write-business-plan, and get started.
- Know what you want to do? Try working for someone else for a while who is in the same business, or even tackling the same customer market. So if you want to set up a souvenir shop in the Lake District, you could probably learn a lot by working in a clothes store in a town in the area. It will show you how many customers are visitors versus locals, and you'll learn all about retail.
- Make sure you have a very detailed cash flow as part of the business plan, then show it to anyone you can find who may have a view. Other people who run (non-competing) businesses are a good start, because they will know all about the importance of accurate cash flows.
- Find the most experienced financial person you can to help and support you. Try finding a mentor – maybe a newly retired accountant?
- If you are going to borrow money from a bank, approach one with your business plan and see how

you get on. Just because one turns you down, it doesn't mean there won't be a bank out there for you. Sometimes you have to kiss a lot of frogs before you find your handsome prince!

## CHAPTER 8

# THE SAVING HABIT

Saving is a habit, just like smoking, and a much more beneficial one to acquire.

Rather like the advice given about the sex in a long-term relationship, which may have become rather sporadic, the important thing is to do it. And eventually you will start to enjoy it.

So let's set up a savings account and get saving.

It really doesn't matter how little. Save £10 a month by standing order into your savings account, and if interest rates average 4 per cent, you will have £1,472.50 in ten years' time. Make that £50, and it will be £7,362.49.

Even better, save 10 per cent of your net pay. If you earn £25,000 a year, your take-home pay every month after tax and national insurance deductions will be £1,651.55. Save 10 per cent of that per year and, even if you don't have a pay rise, after five years you will have saved about £11,000.

## Getting the best interest rate

This needs to be a regular thing that you attend to at least annually, but I would suggest six-monthly. Set a date in your diary to review interest rates and see if you should be swapping to a new account. Rates are low and, although they are predicted to rise soon, they won't rise much for savers.

You should review your savings rates as frequently as you review your credit cards or your mortgage. And then change to get a better rate.

Yes, this takes time and effort – like everything I advocate in this book – but I promise you it is worth it.

## Teaching your children to save

For busy parents, and especially busy working mothers, investing time in training your children about money can be seen as a luxury. But one idea that I like a lot is the four-step method. You give your child £1 per year of their life per week, and then require them to 'allocate' it to four specific areas.

- *Pot 1: charity* – 10 per cent to be spent at the local fête or donated to charity directly.
- *Pot 2: spending money* – 30 per cent can be spent on anything the child wants.
- *Pot 3: something special* – 30 per cent to be saved towards something they really want; every six months the child can spend from this pot.
- *Pot 4: long-term savings* – 30 per cent goes into a bank or building society, to be spent when the child is older.

# ISAs explained

In the UK, if you save into an Individual Savings Account (ISA), the interest on the money is tax free. Because this is a valuable benefit, there are limits regarding how much you can save.

## *Cash ISAs*

If you have an adult ISA (for people aged sixteen and over), the limit in the current year is £5,880 in cash.

Look for the best interest rate. And don't forget to swap to another ISA, if it is offering a better rate in the future.

It may be that you can find a savings account with a better rate than an ISA, even though you will pay tax on the interest.

Here are the sums.

If your ISA is paying 1.5 per cent free of tax, and your savings account is paying 4 per cent but is not tax free, then unless your tax rate is 50 per cent you are better off with the savings account.

Now do it for yourself.

What is the savings account offering (for example, 4 per cent)?

What is your tax rate (for example, 25 per cent)? If you don't know this, consult your pay slip.

Deduct the tax rate from the savings account interest. If it is 25 per cent, you are left with 3 per cent. So you will need to find an ISA paying that, if you want to match the savings account offer.

### Interest rate alert: bonus rates

Banks really want your money, and many of them offer introductory bonuses for the first year you are saving with them. So after you open an ISA, or any savings account, set a date every year to review the rate you will then be getting. See if you can find a better deal elsewhere.

## *Stocks and shares ISAs*

You can also save into an account that invests in stocks and shares. The limit for this is £11,880, although the total limit between the two is also £11,880. So if you want to keep some money in a cash ISA, you have to limit your investment in a stocks and shares ISA.

Again, any income (from dividends) is tax free, and so is any capital gain.

Unlike with cash ISAs, you are risking more because shares go up and down. But for investments being made over a period of five years or longer, most financial advisers tell you to have some exposure to the stock market (because your money could potentially grow by more, if the companies it is invested in do well).

I am fifty-one and don't expect to need my savings until I am at least sixty-five, so I save regularly into a stocks and shares ISA with a company called Fundsmith. Why? Because I understand what they are investing my money in, and – importantly – they charge very low fees.

### Fee alert

Unlike with cash ISAs, the banks and companies who run stocks and shares ISAs charge fees. That makes sense, of course: they have to pay the administration costs of investing your money and then returning it to you when you want to take it back; plus they provide you with a lot more information along the way than you will need if you have a cash ISA.

The fees vary wildly, and it's a good idea to check the small print before committing yourself. I pay a 1 per cent fee at Fundsmith, whereas some high street banks charge 1.75 per cent for their stocks and shares ISAs.

## Investing in the stock market

Over any reasonable length of time, companies who are successful at what they do will grow more rapidly than cash that is sitting in the bank. Buying shares in those companies will therefore almost certainly grow your wealth more comprehensively than money in the bank. That is why people investing your money for the long term – in, for example, your pension – will invest much of it into stocks and shares.

### *Buyer beware*

Okay, this is the deal. Picking who the companies are that will do well is really not much more than informed gambling. The better informed you are, the more successful your gambling will be.

Even when I worked as a stockbroker myself, I rarely invested my own money. (It is a frightening reality that the book I wrote about my time in the world of stocks and shares, *Survival in the City*, has barely dated – that alone should alarm you.)

I have already explained many times in this book how often you should be reviewing the interest rates on your ISAs, your credit cards, your mortgage. These are all very straightforward financial products when compared to buying stocks and shares – and especially compared to other more sophisticated things, such as derivatives.

If you want to make a success of investing in the stock market, you need to be really well informed, all the time, and to know when to buy and sell. Even the people whose job it is to be informed and to buy and sell stocks and shares often don't get it right. No one is infallible. Remember that any investment in the stock market, even if you make it through someone else, is a risk.

If you want to learn how to invest in the stock market, I suggest you do one of these things.

- Join or start a shares club.
- Take a much closer interest in where your pension fund is being invested.
- Follow the fortunes of your employer, if they (or their parent company) are listed on the stock market.

- Invest your money (like I do) with someone else who can devote more time and resources to staying on top of all the information about the companies that are being invested in. As I said, I invest my money into the stock market almost exclusively with Terry Smith at Fundsmith. He's better at picking good investments than anyone else I know, and he has his own money invested in his fund.

But just because you delegate the action, this does not mean that you should delegate the information.

Your pension will be invested in stocks and shares. Do you know which ones? It will be on your statement. I read my Fundsmith statements every six months and log in online from time to time in between.

Make sure you know what your money is being invested in.

## *Starting a shares club*

If ISAs are boring, or you have one already, get together a few of your friends and start a 'shares club', essentially investing your own money on a joint basis. This will make saving fun!

You don't need to be a financial expert, and you can each invest a small amount of money each month. You can register your club – for free – with ProShare (a not-for-profit organization that promotes share ownership in the UK), and then you will be able to track your portfolio online.

### *Trading stocks and shares costs money*

If you really want to do it yourself, open an execution-only account with a cheap online provider (I do this at www.stocktrade.co.uk). When you want to buy some shares in a specific company, because you really believe in them, do it through that account.

I remember Lloyds Banking Group shares being at about 50p in February 2010. I thought that was ridiculously low, and decided to buy some shares then. That investment is looking good, but I made at least two others at the same time that are not.

As I said, trading is risky and best left to the professionals.

## Do you have money somewhere and don't realize it?

I am assuming you have been all round the house and collected every spare coin to put into the savings account I have persuaded you to open. But you may find that you have money you don't even know about, just waiting for some action on your part.

### *Did your children qualify for a child trust fund?*

All children born between 1 September 2002 and 2 January 2011 qualified for a child trust fund and (provided the forms were filled in) were sent a cheque by the government. This benefit has, sadly, now stopped.

At the time, the money was available to everyone who filled in the forms and claimed their child's cheque. If you were not one of those people, the money will have been invested somewhere with your child's name on it, and you should claim it.

Go to https://www.gov.uk/child-trust-funds/overview to find out where the money is.

If you have a child trust fund, you will be able to transfer it to a junior ISA from April 2015, according to current government plans. Make sure you shop around for the best rates and the lowest charges.

## *Do you own some of the £500 million sitting in 'lost' bank accounts?*

It is thought that up to £500 million is sitting in dormant bank accounts (this is not a sleepy bank account; it is simply one that has not been used for about fifteen years or more).

Surprising as it may seem, many of us open bank accounts and then forget about them, or move house, or die, or open accounts for children and don't tell them.

If you want to check if one of these dormant bank accounts is yours, go to https://www.mylostaccount.org.uk.

## *Are you entitled to one of the 898,000 unclaimed Premium Bond prizes?*

Premium Bonds are savings where you don't get any guaranteed return (other than the return of your money), but you do get the chance to win cash prizes that are tax free. It is like playing the lottery but with better odds, and you get your stake money back. Plus, unlike the lottery – where there is a time limit on claiming prizes – there is no time limit on claiming a Premium Bond prize.

Over £44 million is sitting in unclaimed Premium Bond prizes. If you think some of that money may be yours, have a look at http://www.nsandi.com/savings-premium-bonds-have-i-won.

## *Have you got a pension fund somewhere that you have forgotten about?*

Apparently, a quarter of people in the UK with a pension fund have lost their paperwork.

These days, young workers aged between twenty-five and thirty-four have had as many employers as those aged sixty-five or older. One in ten people say the fact that they've moved jobs too many times has made it impossible to keep track of their pensions, while one in five admit to having lost their pension paperwork.

If you think you may have lost track of a pension fund you enrolled in a while ago, you can track it down using the government's online Pension Tracing Service at www.gov.uk/find-lost-pension.

## *Do you have any old banknotes?*

However old they are, the Bank of England (or Scotland) will swap them for new ones. Genuine Bank of England banknotes that have been withdrawn from circulation retain their face value for all time and can be exchanged at the Bank of England in London.

It doesn't cost anything, and banknotes can be exchanged either by post or in person. If you want to apply by post, you can download the form from the website www.bankofengland.co.uk.

If they are really old banknotes, the antique value may be larger than the face value. Do check with a currency dealer, if you think this may be the case.

## *Do you have some old foreign currency notes that went out of circulation years ago?*

Do you still have some French franc notes or some Dutch guilders from before those countries converted to the euro? You can change them with the Currency Commission into euros, US dollars or Canadian dollars.

Visit their website to see which currencies they will change and where you should post the notes to (www.thecurrencycommission.com).

## Saving for the long term

What about saving for the very long-term future, for when you don't – or can't – work any more?

I know I will send you to sleep if I mention the word 'pension', so here is a story instead.

When I fell in love with an Australian and married him, twenty-five years ago, we had bigger questions to answer than, 'Do you take this man/woman to be your lawfully wedded husband/wife?' The more pressing question was, 'Pension or property?'

There are lots of rules and regulations surrounding pensions in the UK. The amount you can save into your pension is limited, and when you turn seventy-five you are required by law to use all the money left in your pension to buy what is known as an 'annuity', unless you can prove that your savings and the state pension combined will give you an income of at least a certain amount (currently £20,000).

What is an annuity? At its most simple, it is a guaranteed amount of money per year for the rest of your life. But in order to get it, you have to hand over your entire pension pot. And if you then die, the money does not return to your estate.

Mr M, coming from 12,000 miles away, never understood why there were so many rules and regulations governing pensions. The thought of being forced to buy an annuity at the age of seventy-five – let alone not being able to leave an asset you had accumulated during your lifetime to your children – was baffling to him.

It was far better, we both reckoned, to make a property investment instead. We married in 1988 and didn't buy the 'pension' until 1999.

Now, in 2013, would we make the same decision again? I think so.

Interest rates are low, and yields are high, which is the best reason for buying property as an investment that I can think of. But here is a golden rule for buying an investment property at any time: remember you are buying an investment, not a home. What will rent?

In my own home I need a gun cupboard, a separate laundry and shelving for a complete collection of post-war *Wisden*. Tenants may happily live without all three.

I had never bought anything except my own home before, and so I turned to my most property-savvy friend, my Medical Girlfriend. She, too, has an Australian husband. And she, too, had gone down the property rather than pension route. I am not too proud to steal other people's ideas, and I recommend you research this kind of thing by asking others!

What was her suggestion?

Buy an investment flat in central London with two bedrooms, two bathrooms and underground car parking, plus a concierge and a river view.

It is in an anonymous brown building that you can only really see if you drive north over Vauxhall Bridge because, although on the riverfront, it is dwarfed by its neighbour, the Panoramic. Like all central London flats, it is leasehold, and the freeholder is the Crown Estate (although Her Majesty has never personally been in touch to ask for the ground rent).

I didn't fall in love with it, or kid myself that it would be our home (or even a pad for our three Cost Centres when they get older and want to be based in London). No, this was strictly a rental proposition.

We had to renovate. My advice is: when renovating, think rental. Two bathrooms are key. And I put down expensive carpets that would bear years of deep cleaning and always come up looking new.

With rates so low, the rent we receive far exceeds the interest on the mortgage, even though the flat was remortgaged to help me buy my business – something else that would have been impossible, if all our assets were in a pension. The flat is jointly owned with Mr Moneypenny, these days a crack cricket coach in Cost Centre #3's school and responsible for the selection and success of the county U14s. All of this occupies him enormously but gives him a much more lenient tax code than me, so we split the income after all the deductions. He gets a much better return than I do.

Theresa is a professional woman in her mid-thirties who works in the asset management business. She, too, bought a property.

‘I got my first proper job when I was twenty-six, and that's when I first took out a pension, because the company offered it to me. I didn't make any contributions myself. The next job, which I held for three years, was with a company that didn't offer me a pension, and I didn't think to take one out myself; I was too young, and wasn't thinking about it. I saw more of an opportunity in property, so I bought a place in Morocco, where my mother lives. ’

## Will you be very poor when you are old?

Think of all the things you would like to do now but can't find the time. When you are older, you may well have the time but not the money!

The really baffling thing to me about pensions is that so many people are offered them by their employer, and decline.

For my TV programme I interviewed a fitness instructor at a gym who was twenty-two and had been working there since he was twenty. Why hadn't he joined the company pension scheme? It would have cost him nothing, and his employer would have paid into it for the previous two years. All it would have taken is a little bit of time to fill in the forms.

His answer was: 'Because I didn't think I was going to stay for long, so it wasn't worth it.'

Wasn't worth it? Free money?

Legislation has overtaken this young man, and now

we have something called auto-enrolment, whereby it will be compulsory for employers to install their employees in a scheme and contribute on their behalf – whether they think it is 'worth it' or not. More than that, the employee will also be required to contribute.

The minimum amount that must, by law, be paid into the pension scheme is 8 per cent of the employee's gross earnings for anyone who earns at least £5,668 and up to £41,450 (these limits will be adjusted each year). Anything you earn above £41,450 isn't taken into account when calculating the compulsory contributions.

So the minimum contribution is 8 per cent. But the minimum the employer has to contribute is 3 per cent. This means that, if your employer contributes only 3 per cent, you will find that 5 per cent of your earnings (between those two figures quoted above) will be diverted, with no choice, into your pension.

Your employer may pay more than 3 per cent – my company, for instance, pays 5 per cent – but you will still have to make up the difference between whatever your employer pays and the 8 per cent required.

## *What to ask your employer*

- When will I be auto-enrolled (every company has an auto-enrolment date)?
- How much of the 8 per cent are you going to contribute, and how much will I have to contribute?

Remember, if your company is only going to pay the minimum (i.e. 3 per cent), you will have to contribute 5 per cent. This is from gross, not net, income. If you don't currently make voluntary contributions, this will seem like an extra tax.

## *What to ask your pension provider*

- Where is my pension invested?

Most people have to choose where their pension is invested when they sign up with the company pension scheme, or set up their own personal pension. They then take very little notice of the arrangements, other than casting a cursory glance at their annual statement. Most people just check the annual amount they will earn in retirement, if certain growth assumptions are met. This figure is an academic illustration, required by law, and it is more fiction than fact (because it is based on so many assumptions).

Typically, Theresa is not overwhelmed by the forecasts on her statement telling her what she may earn in retirement: 'Who the hell knows? Nobody! These figures don't mean anything.'

What you should really be thinking about is where the money is being invested on your behalf (and I say this as someone who has suffered from pension ignorance myself). When you set up a pension plan, you specify the age at which you think you'll need to start receiving an income – you don't have to retire then, it is just a best guess.

Having signed up to the company scheme in 2000, when I was thirty-eight, I probably guessed at a retirement age of sixty. When I turned fifty, the money was automatically taken out of stocks and shares and invested into bonds. I turned fifty in March 2012; between then and when I noticed, the share market has risen and the bond market has performed badly. I have moved it all back into shares now, but that illustrates what happens when you sign a load of forms and don't think about them again for twelve years.

Theresa confessed to me that she doesn't read her annual pension statement. She is charged around £12 a month in management fees, which she can't do anything about, but she can change the funds that she invests in, and she knows that.

‘It's been my new year's resolution for a while now to invest in more sustainable funds. I currently invest in the default fund of UK Equity Index Fund. I know what this means, because I work in this area, but most pension holders don't have any idea how their money is invested.’

If you are like ‘most pension holders’, make it your goal to find out!

Your pension fund is your money. You can't touch it until you retire, so it seems almost irrelevant. But whether you will be rich or poor when you are old depends on action you can take now.

Theresa reflects on what she has achieved in just four years.

❛ Each month I contribute 5 per cent of my gross salary, and the company matches and doubles it. So each month just over £700 goes into my pension. In four years I have accumulated about £38,000. I've read that the rule of thumb is that the percentage of your salary you should be putting aside is what your current age is, divided by two. Perhaps I should be contributing a little more than 5 per cent then, though the company won't match and double anything higher than 5 per cent. ❜

## Women and pensions

Because women take more career breaks, and often work part-time or not at all while raising children, women's pension pots often don't grow as fast as men's.

If I was the one giving up work for a while – whether to follow my partner abroad, or to raise the children – I would be very proactive about topping up my pension pot while I was taking a career break.

Why not ask the partner who is still working if they will save into your pension fund for you? Their pension pot may well not be accessible to you when the time comes, and you should focus on building your own.

## Free money for children!

The government may have taken away the child trust fund cheques, but they still have a way of giving your child money.

If you start a pension for your children, the government will make a contribution to top up whatever you are paying. You don't have to do anything other than open the pension fund with the child's name on it. If, for instance, you save £20 a month into your child's pension (£240 a year), the government will add another £60 per year.

This is worth having, and will help set your children up well for the future.

---

Saving is a habit. Like all habits that are good for you (such as exercise, or eating properly), it will take some discipline and effort to acquire.

Again, time and effort invested by you now will reap enormous rewards in the future.

## Start the saving habit

- *Have you got an ISA?*
  If not, open one with £10. Then set up a standing order to pay a small amount of money in each month. Be ambitious! You can always change it.
- *Do you already have a cash ISA?*
  Try saving into a stocks and shares ISA. But make sure you choose a low fee provider, and remember the value of stocks and shares can go down as well as up.
- *Why not start (or join) a stocks and shares club?*
  Visit the website www.proshareclubs.co.uk to find out all you need to know about setting up and running a successful investment club.
- *Does your company have a Save As You Earn share scheme?*
  If it is a big public company, or part of one, then it may well have. This is where you save money every month into the shares of the company, and the company matches your contribution. It is effectively free money – and because the government wants to encourage such schemes, they don't charge you income tax or national insurance, making your savings grow faster.

What if you have read all these ideas and don't like – or can't do – any of them? But perhaps you still want to learn the savings habit?

Start really small. Challenge yourself to keep every £1 coin you acquire and put it in a tin, then bank the coins at the end of the month.

# CHAPTER 9

# DOING GOOD

Would you like to support good causes but don't know how to start?

This chapter will argue strongly that everyone should be a philanthropist. I will explain how you can become one – even if you have less than no money to give away.

Many people make the argument that those of us lucky enough to have been born into privilege (and remember, half the world thinks running water and sanitation is a privilege) should 'give something back'. You may well already be one of these people. If so, I hope this chapter will show you how to act on your beliefs.

On the other hand, you may feel that you have fought for every penny you own and every privilege you enjoy, and feel no compunction to help those less fortunate than yourself. I also understand this point of view.

If this describes you, I would make a different case for philanthropic activity. I would suggest that by directing your efforts towards making the world a better place, you will learn a great deal that will help you in your own career. Becoming involved with a charity will often afford you the opportunity to learn more skills than you are able to acquire in your main occupation.

And it will help you build relationships you may not

otherwise have. That alone is a good reason to become a philanthropist.

## Donating your wealth takes many forms

At every age and every stage there are things we can all do to help.

I am not an art lover, or an opera lover, or a classical music fan, but I am always ready to be educated by others who are. Thus I found myself taken on a tour of the Museum of Modern Art, in New York City, not long ago by a wealthy (male) benefactor of that collection. He led me from room to room, even getting me to walk into one room with my eyes shut so that when I opened them I enjoyed the full force of one particular painting. (I am not sure even that taught me much – I am such a philistine – but it showed me that I am willing to trust rich and handsome men to lead me around art galleries with my eyes shut.)

What I did notice on the way round MOMA, though, was how many women had donated pieces to the collection. With shocking prejudice I assumed that all these women were wealthy widows who were just handing over pictures and sculptures that their husbands had collected. On further investigation I found out that this was far from the truth.

The most surprising discovery for me was how many

MOMA employees have donated items. Grace M. Mayer, former photography curator, and Greta Daniel, former curator of design, are two of the benefactors (and Daniel also has a fund named after her, which is responsible for many of the objects in the design collection). Alicia Legg was a former sculpture curator of MOMA who worked at the museum for thirty-eight years before retiring, and she has also donated to her former employer.

You don't have to be retired or have moved on from MOMA to be a benefactor; even current employees have given items. Paola Antonelli has given to the collection; she is currently a curator in MOMA's art and design department, and also decides which items make it into the MOMA design shop.

There are some inspirational stories to be uncovered by looking at the female donors to MOMA. In 1980, Barbara Gladstone went from being a forty-year-old, twice-divorced mother of three, teaching art history at Hofstra University, to gallerist – a profession which, at the time, was probably seen as 'suitable for a woman' rather than being the leading career it would be considered today. She now has a gallery named after her: the Gladstone Gallery.

Katherine S. Dreier was an American artist, writer and patron who, like the others listed above, donated items to the collection that came from her own efforts and were not inherited or owned by a family fund. She was very involved in women's suffrage and was a key figure in the development of international modernism in the USA in the 1950s.

And then there are the artists themselves. Louise Bourgeois, for instance. The founder of 'Confessional Art', she is famed for her 'spider sculptures', one of which currently holds the record for being the most expensive work by a female to be sold at auction (at Christie's, in 2011, it sold for $10.7 million). Her donations are from her own studio, so the 'cost' is in labour and the lost earnings from potential sales to an institution or at auction.

These women have all been generous and have effected their bequests through their own efforts, rather than inheriting or marrying money.

## Women play a key part in philanthropic giving

In deciding to contribute towards making the world a better place, at home or abroad, you will be treading in well-worn footsteps. Unlike senior business leaders, most of whom are still male, many leading philanthropists are women and can be looked to as role models.

There are about 165 major women's funds in twenty-seven countries on six continents.

Sisters Helen LaKelly Hunt and Swanee Hunt raised the profile of women's philanthropy with the first Women Moving Millions campaign, which sought million-dollar gifts from women for women's funds around the globe.

The campaign raised $182 million in two years, between 2007 and 2009.

Banking and investment expert Darla Moore made history with her cumulative $70 million gift made between 1998 and 2004 to the University of South Carolina Business School, the first business school in the country to be named for a woman.

There are strong examples of female-led philanthropy on both sides of the Atlantic.

Dame Vivien Duffield has given a total of £400 million to good causes in the UK and Israel over the past thirty years. She has given much of her money through the Clore Duffield Foundation which she runs, focusing on arts and culture for children and young people.

Arianna Huffington, founder of *The Huffington Post*, has called on women to lead 'a third revolution'. She believes that success to date has largely been determined by money and power, so she is calling for 'a third metric' that should be based on 'well-being, wisdom, our ability to wonder, *and to give back*' (my emphasis). 'Don't buy society's definition of success, because it's not working for anyone,' she urged in a speech to Smith College.

## There are many positive benefits to giving

Arianna alludes to the fact that there are benefits to 'giving back'. She's right.

Research has identified eight mechanisms that drive charitable giving. A further study which examined two of these – psychological benefits, and values – may explain why there are significant differences between men and women in their approach to giving.

Because women have been socialized as the caregivers within their families, they may see philanthropy as a means to express their moral beliefs (whereas men, apparently, give because of status and social expectations). Women may experience emotions more strongly than men, and tend to engage in reciprocal behaviour (while men are more competitive).

In conclusion, the study found that women do score significantly higher than men on empathic concern and that women are more likely than men to give, and give more (even when other factors that affect giving are taken into account).

Sara Blakely, founder of the slimming underwear range Spanx, was the first self-made female billionaire to sign up to The Giving Pledge, an initiative by Bill and Melinda Gates and Warren Buffett, which has signed up dozens of the world's billionaires to give away more than half of their wealth (either before or after they die).

Steve Jobs' widow, another billionaire, has now stepped up as a philanthropist. Laurene Powell Jobs is focused on a number of issues, including education and gun control.

In terms of women influencing how charities spend their money, in the USA women hold almost three-quarters of all jobs, and almost half of all CEO positions, in the non-profit sector. But they are woefully under-represented at board and executive level at the really large charities, the ones with more than $25 million in the bank.

In the UK, women occupy 71 per cent of all jobs in the non-profit sector, yet represent only 45 per cent of directors.

## Who should I be giving my money to? And how much?

First of all, consider what you are passionate about.

I am passionate about employability and social mobility, which are inextricably tied up with each other. So my main focus is on work in those areas. I founded the Taylor Bennett Foundation, in 2008, to help black and minority ethnic graduates train and find their first role in communications. This helps minority representation – and thus employability – and also addresses social mobility in the process.

I also chair the employability charity Career Academies UK, which works with young people aged sixteen to nineteen to raise their aspirations and prepare them for the workplace.

Beyond that, I support Sarah Brown's charity Theirworld because she is my dear friend and suffered so much when her daughter, Jennifer, died in 2002. I donate 10 per cent of my UK royalties to her, and a percentage of my box office receipts in Edinburgh.

My advice to you is to determine what interests you, and then find out who is working in that area.

New Philanthropy Capital (www.thinknpc.org) does an excellent job of analysing charities and reporting on whether they are effective places to send your money. If you have a lot of money to give away, they will write a bespoke plan for you.

What about all those people who ask you to sponsor them on bike rides in Patagonia or 5k road races?

You need a policy for this, and then you need to stick to it. My policy is as follows.

If they are a client of my company, then the company gives a specified amount (usually £50). If they are a personal friend, then it is £25.

Your limits may, and will, be different – those £25 donations can add up!

And don't be shy of saying no.

## Not got much money to give away?

Give your time; become a volunteer.

Jane Shepherdson, CEO of Whistles, described how she began volunteering.

“I had always felt there must be something more I could do than just give money to charity, but I assumed my skills were untransferable [sic]. I mean, what use is an eye for a trend in print when dealing with global poverty? I was wrong. Oxfam has a chain of almost seven hundred shops nationwide and wanted to make them more exciting. That I was well equipped to do. I've met loads of women in our industry who are desperate to do something useful, who feel it's the right thing to do – especially those who have been lucky enough to have had some success and want to help those who haven't. I don't see why those activities should be at odds with my professional life. '

People forget that charities are organizations, just like businesses. Oxfam, as Jane realized, has shops. It also has millions of pounds of turnover that needs financial oversight, and lots of employees (including those who volunteer) who need managing. It also needs to recruit people, needs help with interviewing, and it has IT systems that need to be efficient.

Whatever skills and experience you have, it is almost certain that a not-for-profit somewhere will be interested in you.

Referred to as 'soul-offsetting', there is a growing trend of successful women wanting to give back.

BBC newsreader Mishal Husain has signed up to Speakers for Schools, an organization that helps give children at state schools access to the networks enjoyed by those at public schools. She explained her motivation.

' I liked the clear focus on state secondary schools, the effort to match school and speaker, and the potential to influence young people and raise aspirations. I also hope I can be a positive role model for the British Asian community. '

You don't have to be a 'name' to volunteer. It is amazing how many young women, just starting out, are giving back.

In the USA, seven out of ten women entrepreneurs engaged in a new business volunteer their time at least once a month to help community-related causes. In addition, 31 per cent of them contribute $5,000 or more to various charities annually.

Volunteering is also a great way to develop new skills and new contacts.

In addition (as I wrote in my careers advice book), developing a 'third dimension' can give you much-needed topics to discuss with others in semi-social situations.

## The mechanics of giving

Decide what you'd like to give away each year, and then budget for it.

### *Making small donations big*

Crowdfunding is an approach to raising capital for new projects and businesses (for-profit or not-for-profit) by soliciting contributions from a large number of stakeholders. There are three types of crowdfunding models:

- donations, philanthropy and sponsorship (where there is no expected financial return)

- lending, and
- investment (in exchange for equity, profit or revenue sharing).

It's a great way to support budding entrepreneurs and give a boost to the local economy.

Kickstarter, a crowdfunding platform, only launched in the UK at the end of 2012. But in its first six months, a total of thirty-two projects had raised £700,000 in Scotland alone.

While many commercial companies are now using Kickstarter, it also provides an opportunity to fund projects that will make the world a better place, such as the team of scientists at Heriot-Watt University in Edinburgh, who developed a deep-sea diving robot to repair damaged coral reefs. These 'coralbots' scan the seabed for healthy pieces of coral and move them back to the reef, where they re-attach themselves and continue to grow.

Marine biologist Dr Lea-Anne Henry from Heriot-Watt explained that they are also using funds from elsewhere but were astonished at the response from the general public.

'We had such an enormous response to the project when we first started it, we thought, "Let's turn to the public and see what we can do with this avenue." On Kickstarter you offer people rewards, so they can have the feel-good feeling, but they can also have something physical in their hand or something to interact with. I think having that as part of your crowdfunding plan is absolutely key.'

## *Charitable lending*

Microfinance initiative Lendwithcare.org is a scheme that allows people in the UK to lend small sums of money directly to entrepreneurs in the developing world in order to help them grow their businesses.

Sisters Amy and Lucy Smith work part-time at a Co-operative Food store in Hampshire. The 21-year-old identical twins decided to lend money to Esmeralda Nadela, an entrepreneur based in the Philippines wanting to establish a general store in her local community. Amy and Lucy loaned Esmeralda £30.

‘We thought it was a great way of helping people earn a sustainable living, instead of making a one-off donation. When we went online, we were amazed to see farmers, shopkeepers, tailors, all wanting to transform their lives through working and running a business, not through receiving handouts. What's great about the scheme is that, once the loan is repaid, we can recycle it into another loan for another entrepreneur.’

There is a growing interest in this form of giving. New Philanthropy Capital, founded by two partners at Goldman Sachs ten years ago, has written a report on the provision of repayable finance to charities and social enterprises with the aim of creating social impact, and sometimes generating a financial return. This is still a new area, but now grant-making trusts and individual philanthropists are getting involved.

## *Tax-efficient charitable giving*

There are a variety of ways to give to charity, depending on how much and how regularly you are able to give.

It is important to know what tax relief is available on charitable giving, so that both you and the designated charity gain the most from any giving.

In the UK the following works well.

### GIVE AS YOU EARN

Give As You Earn (or payroll giving) is the simplest, most tax-efficient way to give regularly to charity. If your employer offers this option, you can give from your pre-tax gross salary, with tax relief given at source. Alternatively, it may be worth taking out a Charity Account through the Charities Aid Foundation, whereby tax relief is reclaimed automatically and the statement acts as a record of charitable giving, for tax purposes.

### GIFT AID

The Gift Aid scheme increases the value of charitable donations by allowing the charity to reclaim basic-rate tax on the gift. Those who pay tax at 40 per cent and 45 per cent can then reclaim the difference between their tax rate and the basic rate on the total value of the donation. So if you give £100 through Gift Aid to a registered charity, it is grossed up by 20 per cent, which the charity can reclaim, making the value of the gift £120. In the case of a 40 per cent taxpayer, the donor can reclaim the difference between the higher and the basic rate on the grossed-up value.

## GIFT OF ASSETS

A Gift of Assets works in a similar way to Gift Aid. Individuals and companies can claim tax relief when giving certain assets, such as shares and land, to a UK charity. Outright gifts are also free of inheritance tax. Unlike cash donations under Gift Aid, all the tax relief – in this case, capital gains and income/corporation tax – is claimed by the donor. This tax relief is contingent on the donor relinquishing any benefits from the property or land. For example, if you have granted a lease of land to a charity, that lease may count as a 'qualifying interest' in the land. If the lease is rent free or below a market rent, tax relief may be available.

## COMMUNITY DEVELOPMENT FINANCE INITIATIVES/TRUSTS

Where large sums of money are being considered, you may want to invest directly in an existing philanthropic fund or Community Development Finance Institution. CDFIs invest in deprived areas that cannot access mainstream finance. In the case of CDFIs, relief on income and corporation tax is only up to a maximum of 25 per cent of the value of the investment. You can also set up your own company or trust and register it as a charity. This affords you relief on capital gains tax and inheritance tax, and you don't pay tax on the charity's investment income.

Philanthropy Impact (www.philanthropy-impact.org) is a great place to start, if you want some basic information on the different vehicles for giving.

Sir Ian Wood CBE, born in Aberdeen, found that setting up a trust to help young people in Scotland was the most effective way to structure his giving.

'You must get directly involved to give effectively. Good philanthropy shares a lot of the same principles as good business. You can lead by your heart, but your head must come into it too.'

## *Giving shares to charity*

You may not have money to give away, but perhaps you have some worthless shares lying around?

As a result of share splits – or even inheritances – many people end up with small parcels of shares in companies, which it would be uneconomic to sell. You can, however, donate them to charity.

Claire Mackintosh is elegant, educated, articulate and had a successful career in finance before giving it all up to work in the not-for-profit sector. Not a millionaire herself, she nevertheless spotted a gap in the market that allowed her to raise millions of pounds for charity. And even better, it was money that would otherwise be sitting around, not doing anything.

Claire established Sharegift, to convert those uneconomic parcels of shares into cash for charities. Even if you have just one or two shares, it works. Sharegift aggregates them, sells them and then uses the proceeds to make donations to a wide range of other UK-registered charities, based on the suggestions of donors and supporters.

When you donate shares, they are transferred into Sharegift's keeping and placed within their portfolio of shares. Shares are aggregated within the portfolio until there is enough of any one holding to sell. In the meantime, shareholdings may attract dividends or capital payments, and all of this helps create a pool of funds, all of which is donated to charity.

Although you can't specify which charity you want your one share to be donated to, you can nominate charities (or types of charities) that you would like Sharegift to give to in the future. And they will.

If you happen to be a lucky person who has accumulated a lot of shares in one company – through working there for ages, or investment, or inheritance – and you would like to give them away to good causes, or even to a specific good cause, then Sharegift can help with that as well.

## Legacies

Should you give all your money to your children?

Richard Branson, Bill Gates and Warren Buffett have all said that they would rather invest most of their fortunes in helping society. 'I definitely think leaving kids massive amounts of money is not a favour to them,' Gates told *The Huffington Post* in early 2013.

The billionaire philanthropist Warren Buffett, then seventy-six, was interviewed in 2006 by *Fortune* on why he felt so strongly about limiting the amount of personal wealth you pass on to your children.

> ' I would argue that when your kids have all the advantages anyway – in terms of how they grow up and the opportunities they have for education, including what they learn at home – I would say it's neither right nor rational to be flooding them with money. '

Instead, Buffett has given his children money to set up foundations which give money back to society. 'And they aren't just writing cheques,' he explained, 'they've put enormous thought and effort into the process.'

Perhaps surprisingly, about half of us never make a will.

Why not go to Will Aid for help with drafting your will? This is a charity which donates the fee you pay to one of nine charities. The suggested donation is £90 for a basic single will, and £135 for a pair of basic mirror wills. By 2013, the charity had raised £13.6 million for good causes over the course of twenty-five years.

Currently, only 7 per cent of those who do make wills leave anything to charities – although 75 per cent regularly donate to good causes – according to Remember a Charity, an organization set up to boost legacy income.

There is a tax benefit to giving away even a relatively small portion of your fortune. If you want to bequeath money to charity in your will, it is paid out before the size of the estate is assessed for inheritance tax purposes. As of 6 April 2012, if you bequeath 10 per cent or more of your estate, you will pay a reduced rate of 36 per cent (rather than 40 per cent) on the remainder of the estate liable for inheritance tax.

A study by the government's Behavioural Insights Team in mid-2012 found that people are more likely to donate via a will if prompted to do so by their solicitors. Also, suggesting that charitable giving is common practice and asking people to choose a charity makes it more likely that a donation will be added to a will, and also that it will be bigger.

## Money you'd spend anyway: responsible spending

Juliet Davenport, CEO of Good Energy, was awarded an OBE in 2013 for her work.

‘ At Good Energy, we're trying to make the market a place where renewable energy can flourish. Our ambition is to help individuals be more responsible for their own energy; using energy wisely not only means spending less money, but doing less harm to the environment, too.

We know the price point is very important for customers. When we started, we were 10 per cent more expensive than non-renewable electricity providers. Now we're much more competitive – usually costing less than the Big Six's standard dual fuel tariffs. We're always trying to give value for money. It's important to us that people understand going green doesn't have to be a luxury they can't afford. ’

I am a cynic when it comes to happiness, and don't believe it should be anyone's specific goal – on the grounds that, if it is, you are bound to be disappointed, as no one can be happy all the time. But contentment is a reasonable goal and, for some people, spending responsibly can help them sleep better at night.

The responsible consumer is someone who 'knows' what they are buying – knows what it has taken to produce that item or service – because not 'knowing' leads to abuse and exploitation of people and the natural world.

If this matters to you – and to many of you it will – then it is always worth asking the companies you support with your precious money some basic questions about how they treat their livestock, how they treat their workers (all the way down the supply chain to the farmer in Costa Rica), whether they have an environmental policy, and whether they support local charities.

In my own office, by way of example, we deliberately chose to get our water machines from a company that donates a portion of its profits to Water Aid. And two of those machines simply chill tap water, thereby reducing the amount of water that has to be transported to us by road.

# Doing good at work

Are women 'greener' and more concerned with sustainability in the workplace than men?

Research from Net Impact's 2012 Talent Report suggests this is the case.

And a GreenBiz analysis in 2013 showed how much women, in particular, are already doing. Indeed, working women are more likely to put a higher premium on working for an organization that is concerned with its ethical and social commitments.

If you want to improve the company or organization you work for, you can do that – even as the lowliest employee, you can still influence for the better the way in which your company spends its money. (For example, my staff were the deciding factor when it came to buying water for the office.)

In their book *Making Good*, authors Dev Aujla and Billy Parish suggest the following action points for employees who want to help change things for the better in society. Each action point makes financial sense; either because it's about efficiency, which is good for the bottom line, or because it improves the company's image, which is good for business.

- *Change the way your company buys stuff.* Get your company to purchase its stationery, toner and office furniture from companies that are seeking to reduce their environmental impact. Start with something simple, such as paper. (By the way, a 'good' product doesn't necessarily mean it's more expensive.)

- *Make something efficiently good*. Every industry could cut down on its waste – waste that costs companies energy, time and resources. Rethink the potential of this waste and repurpose it for good, all the while making it more efficient.
- *Be an industry translator*. Every industry has a language, a lexicon, and a way of thinking. Speak with a community group that is working to change something in your industry, and give them advice on framing their issue.
- *Ask good questions*. Ask your suppliers or partners about their labour practices, or what they are doing to be more environmentally friendly. Just making it clear that this is something your company cares about can spur them to try to justify themselves and do some good – even if you don't have approval from higher up.
- *Get your company to go carbon neutral*. Companies can save a lot of money by being more energy efficient. Talk to operations, talk to the corporate social responsibility (CSR) department, or send an email to your boss. Tell them you are interested in pushing this forward in the company.

Even those of us with very little money can be meaningful philanthropists.

Philanthropy should be part of everyone's life. Even if you are the most selfish person on the planet, and would never consider giving your money and time to others, you should do so anyway. Consider all the career benefits it will bring (and which I outlined in my book about careers advice): personal development, broadening of skills, expansion of your social capital.

But most of us will want to make the world a better place. And every one of us can do so, however little money we have.

## HOMEWORK FOR INDEPENDENT WOMEN

# Good work

- *Identify the good causes that you would like to help, whether with your time or your money.*
  Read more about the charities involved, and follow them on Twitter. Then write and offer your support, and ask what volunteer opportunities are available. It is best to attach your CV or outline your specific skills, and also to state in what capacity you would prefer to serve.

  Some charities have minimum requirements. If, for instance, you volunteer your time at Battersea Dogs and Cats Home in London, you may be asked to do nice-sounding jobs (such as dog walking and cat stroking). But you must complete twenty hours of training and then you must turn up on the same day each week for at least four hours, promise to commit for at least six months, and have an attendance record of at least 75 per cent.
- *Agree a giving budget with yourself (or your partner, if you have one).*
  I would suggest that even the least well off should consider giving £12 a year, or £1 a month. Such a small sum can be organized through a debit or even a credit card.

- *Give away a proportion of your assets.*
  If you are in the fortunate position of having assets, and you have the services of a private banker or an investment adviser, make an appointment to see them and discuss how you can give a proportion of your assets away effectively.
- *Make a will and specify a bequest to a charity.* This could be as little as £100. Even better, do this via Will Aid which organizes local solicitors to write wills for free every November, in return for a donation to charity.
- *Download 'Donor Q&A' from New Philanthropy Capital.*
  Visit http://www.thinknpc.org/publications/donor-qa/ to download this free publication. The booklet is designed to provide practical advice for first-time and experienced donors alike, from choosing a cause to identifying charities operating in your area of interest and evaluating their success.

  It also helps you consider how long to fund a charity for, and suggests ways to ease the transition when you decide to withdraw your support.

  The final section answers questions about becoming a charity trustee and setting up a charitable trust for those looking for more hands-on engagement, as well as addressing some of the thornier issues (such as administration costs and giving during a recession).

CHAPTER 10

# BEING PREPARED FOR WHEN THINGS DON'T GO TO PLAN

Sometimes words are not enough.

I used plenty of them ten years ago, when my Single Girlfriend still had not found Mr Right.

In the end, I realized that action, rather than words, was the motto of the day. So I decided to take her with me to meet as many single men as possible.

I started, on 9 February 2004, by taking her to a party thrown by my friend the Eligible Banker (eligible because solvent, not married and not gay). The party was to celebrate his management buyout and, though he shook my Single Girlfriend's hand, no words were exchanged.

I resorted to fixing a double dinner date with Single Girlfriend, me, Eligible Banker and a former client of his.

This time, words were exchanged; in fact, they talked well into the night.

But then it looked for a while as if words were all that their relationship would amount to. They met for coffee a few times, and even went to the cinema, but nothing happened.

'What's wrong with you?' I demanded of my Single Girlfriend. 'Just jump on him!' I threatened to sign her up to an internet dating site, if he stopped seeing her.

I invited them both to join me at an evening function

in a Mayfair hotel. She looked beautiful and he looked gorgeous in black tie, as most men do. When he left, she saw him out.

'Why did you bother?' I demanded when she returned, a while later.

Her reply showed me that Eligible Banker had finally abandoned talking for action. 'I didn't want to stop snogging him,' she replied.

One of the reasons I was convinced that they would get on well was that they were both chartered accountants. He had qualified with Touche Ross in Leeds, she with KPMG in Sydney.

This proved to be both the glue and the friction in their relationship. Neither could agree who was the senior partner. Long after they had fallen in love, had a baby and bought a house, they were still in dispute about which bathroom tiles to buy for their en suite.

They moved in together in spring 2005. Or rather, she moved in with him. I helped her move. Until then, I had never stopped to consider just how much stuff a bachelor can amass if he remains unmarried into his late thirties. There was nowhere for my girlfriend's kitchen equipment, her shoe collection looked destined for a bin liner, and as for anywhere to put her cosmetics . . .

One more baby and, even in a new house, space was at a premium. He was particularly resistant to the idea of flogging his spherical bookcase on eBay, so my girlfriend once again forged a compromise; it now sat in the children's room with clothes, books and toys on it (testament to who really was the senior partner).

He came to see me at the end of January 2009 and, after talking shop for a few minutes, he asked me to drop by and spend some time with my girlfriend. He was going to South Africa for a week on business, and he thought she might be lonely.

She herself called me three days later. But her words were overwhelmed by tears.

And when I made it back from my business trip the next day, to be by her side, we didn't use words at all. We just held each other and cried.

Eligible Banker had collapsed and died while out walking on Table Mountain, one day short of the fifth anniversary of their first meeting. He was forty-four.

Five years later, my Single Girlfriend is still single and raising his boys as he would wish. They are wonderful children. I love them dearly, and wish I saw more of them. But one thing I also wish is that their father had made a will.

He didn't expect anything to happen to him; he was forty-four, with no health issues, and in good shape. He had enjoyed hiking up mountains from his childhood and university days in Yorkshire. So he hadn't made a will.

More than half the people in the UK don't have a will. If I get you to do one thing as a result of reading this book, this would be a good one to do.

If you are in a relationship with someone, and you are not married, then it is really, really important. My friends, who were engaged and had two children, had not got round to getting married. That is why I wish he had made a will. Without one, life is so much tougher for the person left behind, which is not what anyone wants.

If you are not married, the surviving partner can end up with nothing (other than a share of any joint assets). And even if you are married, or in a civil partnership, if you die without making a will only a certain amount will go to your partner.

If you want things to happen the way you would like them to, please make a will.

It is a salutary statistic that, last year, the UK government benefited from more than £8 million as a result of people not making a will.

You can make a will very cheaply. Lots of people go to a solicitor, but there are several ways of doing it.

- *Use the internet.* You can download a sample will from the internet and adjust it to reflect your wishes. (However, many people caution against this, just in case it turns out not to be valid.)
- *Contact a charity.* Several charities offer a will-making service cheaply, or even for free, in return for you leaving them a donation when you die. Every November, a charity called Will Aid works with local solicitors all over the country to write wills for people for free, in exchange for a donation to charity. If it is not November, you can register with them at www.willaid.org.uk and they will get in touch with you when they start their campaign in September.
- *Use a will-writing service.* This tends to be cheaper, but they may also ask to be the executors of your

will, which means there could be hefty fees to pay when the time comes. That won't be your concern, of course, but given that you are doing this as a favour for the people left behind, it's best to think about it carefully. That caveat also applies to banks, many of whom also offer a will-writing service.

- *Use a local solicitor*. This may not be as expensive as you think. And it certainly won't be nearly as expensive as the situation you may leave behind for your nearest and dearest to resolve, if anything happens to you.

Don't forget, whatever you want to happen needs to be written down. This includes any personal requests (for example, concerning specific items of jewellery). You can also specify what you wish to happen to your children, if they are left with no surviving parent. There is a very useful guide to all this on the Consumers' Association website.

## Do I need life insurance?

I made a will as soon as I had some life insurance, at the age of twenty-one. I realized that, if I died, it would pay out, and I wanted to make sure it did so in accordance with my wishes.

The minute that someone depends on you in any way, you should make a will. And you should also think about taking out life insurance.

Not everyone needs to take out life insurance. Wonderful Wayne, my single safety pilot, currently has no dependents. If he ever writes himself off with his plane, while we would all be very sad indeed, no one would be left without a roof over their head or in serious financial difficulties as a result of his demise.

By contrast, I know that Mr M and the Cost Centres would be materially worse off, if anything happened to me. So I insure my life for enough money to pay off the remaining part of our mortgage, get the children through the rest of their education, and give Mr M a bit of a buffer on the golf club membership fees.

Your employer will almost certainly have arranged life insurance for you. Do you know how much it is for? Have you signed a letter of wish stating who the payout will go to, if anything happens to you?

Life insurance is a very straightforward product, and there is a lot to be said for shopping around for the cheapest premium. A premium is usually for a fixed period of time, after which you will have to renew it. Many companies will require you to have life insurance if you have a mortgage.

## What else do I need to insure?

### *Your car*

The law requires you to insure your car. However, it does not require you to insure it with the same company each year.

Many people simply accept the renewal notice each

year and continue with the same insurer, without comparing prices.

Don't be one of them!

## *Your house and contents*

If you have a mortgage, the bank lending money to you will require you to insure your house. They will not require you to insure your contents, but you can usually get a much better deal for house contents if you insure the building and contents together.

Again, like insuring your car, it is important to shop around every time the renewal comes up.

## *Your pets*

I am the proud owner of two Labradors (a black and a yellow), and I am not alone – currently, almost half of us own pets.

While we're happy to spend on average £365 a year grooming and treating our dogs, and on average £418 a year buying cat food, when it comes to pet insurance most of us don't bother.

But I do. Both animals have been insured since they arrived with us.

The black Labrador came from a local breeder and the yellow one, her son, was from the litter of puppies I delivered in our kitchen one New Year's Eve. (What terrible timing. I could hear the fun everyone was having in the pub next door all the way through the big event!)

I insure my pets because vet's bills are expensive, and getting more so. They are rising on average by 34 per cent a year. Can you afford to treat your pet, if it gets seriously sick or has an accident? If the answer is no, buy insurance.

Remember to shop around. Looking right now for a year's insurance on a Labrador puppy, I found quotes from £179 to £660.

### *Your white goods*

These days the reliability of 'white goods' (fridges, freezers, washing machines, dryers) and electronics (TVs, computers) is so good that the extended warranties on offer are frequently very expensive and unnecessary. At certain ages you have a much higher chance of dying than you have of your white goods or electronic items breaking down. Rather than taking out extended warranties on these items, consider taking out one policy to cover everything in your home (with someone like Protect Your Bubble). Alternatively, you could add it all to your contents insurance.

## A word of caution – a note on joint finances

Different people have different ideas about joint finances, and I am not here to pronounce on what is best. It will be whatever works best for you.

Some couples put everything into a joint account. It is all 'their' money (which is what we do).

Others have separate accounts and just have a joint account for common expenses.

What constitutes 'joint' expenses is an interesting argument, and a debate that I know many couples have. (I even know of one wife who persuaded her husband to pay her waxing bill from their joint account, on the basis that he benefited just as much as she did.)

I have always counselled women who give up work to have their own bank account – to pay for presents, trips to the hairdresser, etc. But where is the money in this account to come from?

If you have savings, then obviously that is one source. But if you have given up work to raise a family, and it is a joint decision, I would argue strongly that you allocate money for yourself when working out the joint family budget. It is very un-empowering to go from bringing in the money to having to ask someone else's permission for every penny you spend.

Equally, think about your pension.

There is nothing to stop the joint budget including a contribution to your pension, as well as his. And if you are the one going out to work while he is staying home – as will happen much more frequently in the future – the reverse applies.

## *Before you jump – get a prenuptial agreement*

I have been married for twenty-five years. But I never take a single day for granted, as 42 per cent of marriages in England and Wales are expected to end in divorce.

I had a prenuptial agreement, even when I was an almost penniless 26-year-old.

Why?

For two reasons.

I owned some valuable art that I didn't want to leave with my husband, if the marriage failed. And also – and, perhaps, more importantly at the time – my husband's previous marriage had ended with a division of personal assets (essentially the wedding presents) that aroused some critical comment from others.

As a sensitive girl in her twenties, I was keen to show that, even if the marriage failed, I would not be leaving with any of his possessions, or he with mine. And so we signed a prenuptial contract.

We were married in Hong Kong, and the argument I have heard against prenuptial agreements is that they are not enforceable in the UK. That is not strictly true – and, in any event, any court would take into account the wishes of the couple at the time they entered into such an agreement.

If you are thinking of getting married, or entering into a civil partnership, or even cohabiting, I would think seriously about having an agreement between you regarding what will happen if you break up.

## *Marriage and business*

If you go into business with your partner, you must think about what will happen to the company in the event of divorce.

Government statistics from 2012 show that families own 62 per cent of Britain's 1.2 million small employers.

In the event of divorce, a court will always try to make a clean break between the couple. Therefore, one partner will be leaving the business, taking cash or other assets with them. These can include things with no obvious monetary value, such as their skills and goodwill, which can have a very negative impact.

An article in the *Sunday Times* featured Phil and Karen Gilbert, who jointly own their 1960s-style diner and continue to run their company despite separating after twenty-five years of marriage. 'We had no alternative but to keep going,' he said. 'We have both put everything into the business. We can't bear to let it crumble, and we certainly can't afford to buy one another out.' Interestingly, he went on to say that 'she knows I rely on her'.

Couples can draw up shareholder agreements that set out how they will divide their responsibilities and assets in the event of divorce (essentially prenuptial agreements for businesses).

Amazingly, most don't.

Many husbands and wives become directors in their spouse's business for tax purposes, with little day-to-day involvement. That distance can make it harder for them to consider the firm's future when a relationship breaks down. It is claimed that this can result in spouses spending thousands of pounds on forensic accountants to find out how much they can claim in a settlement.

So before you take a formal part in any family business – however small – make sure you find out what will happen if the relationship ends.

No one likes to think that things will go wrong.

But they can.

And when they do, they can cause massive financial headaches for everyone.

If you want to protect yourself and everyone around you from the consequences of things going wrong, make sure you have the arrangements in place.

And above all, make a will.

## HOMEWORK FOR INDEPENDENT WOMEN

# Put the arrangements in place

- *Have you made a will?*
  If not, please make one. Write down a list of everyone who you want to benefit, then find a local solicitor (or a charity) that will make a will for you.
- *If you have made a will, has anything changed since you made it?*
  Have you got married, separated, divorced, had children? Every time something changes in your life, you need to change your will.
- *Do you have life insurance with your employer?*
  If the answer is yes, do you know how much it is? If the answer is no, do you need to take some out to protect those who are dependent on you? Use a price comparison website to check out the cheapest rates.
- *Are your pets insured?*
  If not, get a quote from a price comparison website and see how inexpensive it can be to protect yourself from horrendous vet's bills.

# EPILOGUE

This book was designed as a call to action, and the person it was calling to is you.

Now that you have read it, what information are you going to seek out?

And what are you going to do with that information when you have it?

The truth is that the steps which stand between you and the complete mastery of your financial future are not many. But they require the investment of that most precious resource of all – time.

If you take my advice, and invest the time, I promise it will be an investment that will reap the greatest reward of all – peace of mind. Nothing, but nothing, feels as good as the knowledge that you have your financial goals established and under way.

And remember, as the late Helen Gurley Brown, long-time editor of *Cosmopolitan* magazine and herself a famed champion of women's choice, once said: 'Money, if it does not bring you happiness, will at least help you be miserable in comfort.'

# ACKNOWLEDGEMENTS

While I am responsible for all errors and omissions in this book, I could not have written it without the help of many people.

Anya Hart Dyke was once again my intrepid researcher, working remotely in Edinburgh, and it is a measure of how long the project has been under way that she managed to get engaged, married and conceive her first child between commission and publication. Truly valiant multitasking.

A special thanks also goes to the lovely Betsy Mead, a recent Harvard graduate, who helped Anya with some of our US research.

I wrote the manuscript during a family holiday in Australia, and I have to thank my eldest son, Robert McGregor, and my eldest sister-in-law, Jane McGregor, for reading several versions of draft chapters. Plus the rest of my family for leaving me in peace to get on with it.

Caro Moses and Anne Ashworth also provided me with some very last-minute help and support at a crucial juncture, and their readiness to drop everything to help me with no notice at all tells you a lot about how much I lean on my friends and how wonderful they are in responding to cries for help!

I am blessed with a team at Penguin who have helped and encouraged me when I wondered if I would ever have time to write this book. This is a book written for women, by a woman, and given that publishing is a largely female-dominated industry, I am always amazed that I have both a male editor and a male publicist. Joel Rickett, my editor, never shouted at me when I had deadline issues and, indeed, came up with some very interesting anecdotes that have made their way into the book. Richard Lennon also was constantly supportive in helping me balance the demands of my day job with doing much more interesting things like attend book festivals. Alison Alexanian put a lot of energy into supporting both them and me.

An author has to do a lot of work between the acceptance of a manuscript and the publication of a book. Anna de Winton, gap-year student extraordinaire, provided me with very valuable support during this time.

But the final, and perhaps the biggest, thanks go to Caroline Michel. Despite not formally representing me, she encouraged me to write a follow-on to *Careers Advice for Ambitious Women* and made the key phone call that was needed to get me started. She is not referred to in my newspaper column as my Most Influential Girlfriend for nothing.

# NOTES

CHAPTER 1: YOUR FINANCIAL GOALS (or MONEY IS NOT BORING)

page 15 **While the longevity gap ... X chromosome.** 'Catching up: In the rich world men are closing the longevity gap with women'. 12 January 2013. *Economist*.

page 15 **The entrepreneur says ... multi-million-pound company.** Victoria Ward. 'Cath Kidston: "I do not aspire to be a housewife"'. 21 April 2013. *Telegraph*.

page 16 **Jemima Khan ... will inherit.** 'News Review' opinion piece by Jemima Khan. 21 April 2013. *Sunday Times*.

page 16 **Women in their fifties ... the workforce as a whole.** 'Gender pay gap twice as large for women in their fifties'. TUC report dated 19 February 2013. http://www.tuc.org.uk/equality-issues/gender-equality/gender-pay-gap-twice-large-women-their-50s.

page 17 **At the time of writing ... 15 per cent of men.** Carolyn Saunders. 'Pot half full? How women lose out when it comes to pensions'. 1 May 2013. *Guardian*.

page 17 **Over 2.2 million working mums ... primary breadwinner for her family.** Dalia Ben-Galim and

Spencer Thomson. *Who's Breadwinning? Working Mothers and the New Face of Family Support*. 2013. London: Institute for Public Policy Research.

## CHAPTER 2: CUTTING THE COST OF EVERYDAY LIFE

**page 46 Research from the Office for National Statistics ... in reverse.** 'Poor spend £1 in every £4 on housing and energy'. 4 December 2013. *Telegraph*.

**page 46 This was confirmed by Barnardo's ... energy and food.** Nicola Smith and Ivan Mathers. 2013. *The Real Cost of Living*. Ilford: Barnardo's. Available to download from http://www.barnardos.org.uk/the_real_cost_of_living.pdf.

**page 47 Unsurprisingly, a Which? Quarterly Consumer Report . . . food prices (75 per cent).** See http://www.which.co.uk/news/2012/07/we-spend-a-week-a-year-worrying-about-money-291741/. Visited 3 February 2014.

**page 50 In early 2012 ... better interest rate on their savings.** In the UK 1,500 adults aged 18 to 64 were interviewed in early 2012 by Claire Barratt and Katie Taylor of Lloyds Bank TSB. '"Money Mummies" Are Taking Control of the Family Purse Strings' is available to download from http://www.lloydsbankinggroup.com/media/pdfs/LTSB/2012/2809_mummies.pdf.

**page 51 So it's no wonder research has shown . . . finishing your contract early.** Zoe Kleinman. 30 March 2013.

'Counting data cost on mobile phones'. See http://www.bbc.co.uk/news/technology-21959032.

page 52 **One report found ... energy-efficient appliances.** See the 'Watts in the Kitchen' report, available to download from http://globalactionplan.org.uk/node/1050.

page 55 **If you really want to stretch your culinary abilities ... nutritious.** Kevin Rawlinson. 'The single mother who turned 9p meals into a publishing deal with A Girl Called Jack blog'. 10 May 2013. *Independent.*

page 57 **I say this because a study in the USA ... offered the same rate.** Rosemary Bennett. 'Sexist rip-off garages and how to beat them'. 20 July 2013. *Times.*

page 60 **Random fact: in Denmark ... for long hair.** Bim Adewunmi. 'The sexual politics of hair – are all cuts created equally?' 22 January 2013. *Guardian.*

page 61 **In 2011, a study was done in the USA ... price disparities.** Megan Duesterhaus, Liz Grauerholz, Rebecca Weichsel and Nicholas A. Guittar. 2011. 'The cost of doing femininity: Gendered disparities in pricing of personal care products and services'. *Gender Issues*, 28 (4), 175–91.

## CHAPTER 3: PROPERTY (OR HOW TO SPEND A LOT OF MONEY)

page 69 **A Halifax report in July 2012 revealed ... 30 per cent).** Alex Johnson. 'The differences between women and men'. 9 July 2012. *Independent.*

**page 70 At the beginning of 2013, around 31 per cent ... over the same period.** Michelle McGagh. 'Is buying rental property better than a pension?' 28 March 2013. Citywire Money ('The Lolly') website. http://citywire.co.uk/money/is-buying-rental-property-better-than-a-pension/a669820.

**page 73 In October 2012 ... a median of £49,000.** See http://www.staticwhich.co.uk/documents/pdf/quarterly-consumer-report-october-2012-299958.pdf. Visited 3 February 2014.

**page 73 Of the 85,035 homeowners ... nearly half of them were women.** The Consumer Credit Counselling Service (CCCS) changed its name in December 2012 to StepChange Debt Charity. See www.stepchange.org. Visited 3 February 2014.

**page 74 The high barriers to first-time property purchase ... fifteen-year low).** Lee Boyce. 'Mortgage approvals slump to a 15-year low as property purchases dive by a fifth'. 24 July 2012. This is Money website. http://www.thisismoney.co.uk/money/mortgageshome/article-2178225/BBA-mortgage-approvals-slumped-15-year-low-June.html.

**page 78 Back in 2000, I would have been lucky ... 6 per cent.** See official bank rate history at http://www.bankofengland.co.uk/boeapps/iadb/repo.asp. Visited 3 February 2014.

**page 97 However, another sensible way to approach it ... the fee is £199).** Visit http://mortgageadvisers.which.co.uk/. Visited 3 February 2014.

**page 98 But I can tell you that a really useful checklist . . . worth watching.** See the video at http://www.theguardian.com/money/video/2013/may/09/how-to-buy-a-house-video. Visited 3 February 2014.

CHAPTER 4: DEALING WITH DEBT

**page 105 On average, households in the UK . . . borrowed money.** See http://www.staticwhich.co.uk/documents/pdf/quarterly-consumer-report-october-2012-299958.pdf. Visited 3 February 2014.

**page 105 Debt levels are at their highest since the 1980s . . . levels of debt.** 'We spend a week a year worrying about money: Britain on the edge when it comes to finances'. 24 July 2012. Which? News website. http://www.which.co.uk/news/2012/07/we-spend-a-week-a-year-worrying-about-money-291741/.

**page 106 They make up over 75 per cent . . . paying off a loan.** Maha Atal. 'Bringing microfinance to America may be harder than you think'. 5 November 2012. *Forbes*.

**page 108 A solar lamp that lasts for years . . . no one will lend it to them.** Tim Smedley. 'Sustainable technologies: finding financing models that work'. 13 December 2012. *Guardian*.

**page 111 A survey of 700 women . . . when relationships are not going well.** Karen J. Pine. 2009. *Sheconomics Survey Report*. Hatfield: University of Hertfordshire. Available to download from http://www.sheconomics.com/downloads/womens_emotions.pdf.

**page 111 A 2011 study in the USA . . . bail out their exes, too.** 'The 7 Money Mistakes Women Make More Than Men'. 1 May 2012. *Huffington Post*.

**page 112 Apparently, one in ten mothers . . . at home with their newborn.** Jennifer Tippett. 'We wanted to be with our babies . . . but debts forced us back to work early'. 24 April 2012. *Sun*.

**page 112 Almost six in ten . . . want to continue their careers.** According to a study carried out in 2012 by uSwitch. See http://www.uswitch.com/blog/2012/09/07/money-worries-forcing-new-mums-back-to-work- early/. Visited 3 February 2014.

**page 114 Yogeeta Mistry is an elegant . . . to an absolute minimum.** Jon Griffin. 'Birmingham woman wiped out £33,000 debt to run £2m-a-year franchise'. 2 November 2012. *Birmingham Mail*.

**page 127 In the USA, 20 per cent of women . . . to pay off educational debt.** Meghan Casserly. 'The student loan debt crisis is a women's issue: Here's why'. 19 November 2012. *Forbes*.

**page 127 Even with the same qualifications . . . their male counterparts.** Christianne Corbett and Catherine Hill. 2012. *Graduating to a Pay Gap: The Earnings of Women and Men One Year After College Graduation*. Washington, DC: American Association of University Women. Available to download from http://www.aauw.org/files/2013/02/graduating-to-a-pay-gap-the-earnings-of-women-and-men-one-year-after-college-graduation.pdf.

**page 130 Energy comparison site uSwitch . . . fewer than 4 million in 2012.** Lauren Vasquez. 'Collective consumer debt to energy suppliers tops £637m: An estimated 20% are in debt to their provider an average of £123'. 9 April 2013. uSwitch.com website. http://www.uswitch.com/gas-electricity/news/2013/04/09/collective-consumer-debt-to-energy-suppliers-tops-637m/.

**page 131 In autumn 2012, Which? found . . . a new credit or store card).** See http://www.staticwhich.co.uk/documents/pdf/quarterly-consumer-report-october-2012-299958.pdf. Visited 17 January 2014.

**page 131 In practice, despite the avalanche . . . all other loans.** According to the author's email correspondence with Wonga, 7 May 2013.

**page 133 An IVA allows you to repay . . . all charges and interest are frozen.** See http://www.ivaonline.co.uk/. Visited 17 January 2014.

**page 134 You can only get an IVA . . . each time you make a payment.** See https://www.gov.uk/options-for-paying-off-your-debts/individual-voluntary-arrangements. Visited 17 January 2014.

**page 134 The idea is to prioritize your debts . . . overdrafts and bank loans.** 'How to prioritise your debt – priority and non-priority debts'. The Money Advice Service website. https://www.moneyadviceservice.org.uk/en/articles/how-to-prioritise-your-debts. Visited 17 January 2014.

**page 135 Some debt management companies will charge . . . each time you make a payment.** See https://www.gov.uk/options-for-paying-off-your-debts/debt-management-plans. Visited 17 January 2014.

**page 135 However, there are also charities . . . for free.** 'Options for clearing your debts – England and Wales'. The Money Advice Service website. https://www.moneyadviceservice.org.uk/en/articles/options-for-clearing-your-debts-england-and-wales. Visited 17 January 2014.

**page 136 You may also have to make monthly payments . . . for up to three years.** The system is different in Northern Ireland and Scotland. Citizens Advice can tell you if there are any charities which can help you pay the fees. See https://www.gov.uk/bankruptcy/overview. Visited 17 January 2014.

**page 137 Research has shown that the hunt for and use of credit . . . women of all classes.** Beverly Lemire, Ruth Pearson and Gail Grace Campbell. 2001. *Women and Credit: Researching the Past, Refiguring the Future*. Oxford: Berg Publishers.

**page 137 The Equal Credit Opportunity Act . . . credit-granting decisions.** Gail Cunningham. 'The history of women and credit'. Military.com website. http://www.military.com/money/personal-finance/credit-debt-management/the-history-of-women-and-credit.html. Visited 17 January 2014.

## CHAPTER 5: GETTING FINANCIALLY LITERATE

**page 141 It is literacy, not maths, which transforms ... and why?').**Victoria Pynchon. 'How financial literacy can transform women's lives'. 11 February 2011. *Forbes*.

**page 142 People with low financial literacy ... plan for retirement.** Annamaria Lusardi, Olivia S. Mitchell and Vilsa Curto. 2010. 'Financial literacy among the young'. *Journal of Consumer Affairs*, 44 (2), 358–40.

**page 143 The OECD's financial education programmes ... developed countries too!** See the website of the Organisation for Economic Co-operation and Development. http://www.oecd.org/education/. Visited 17 January 2014.

**page 143 Women seem to be hesitant ... salaries measure up.** 'Women and finance'. 1 April 2010. *International Business Times* online. http://www.ibtimes.com/women-finance-190383.

**page 143 Experts say that many women ... purchasing decisions.** Tara Siegel Bernard. 'Financial advice by women for women'. 23 April 2010. *New York Times*.

**page 143 The Personal Finance Education Group ... consumer rights education in schools.** For more information see http://www.pfeg.org/introduction-what-financial-education. Visited 17 January 2014.

**page 150 There are 12,000 of these in the UK, according to ProShare ... will grow.** For more information see http://

www.proshareclubs.co.uk/cgi-bin/proshareclubs/startingaclub/starting.cgi. Visited 17 January 2014.

**page 151 The 'key elements' are . . . behaviour change).** For more information on the Department for International Development's education programmes see their website. https://www.gov.uk/browse/citizenship/international-development/country-regional-funding. Visited 17 January 2014.

## CHAPTER 6: EARNING MORE

**page 158 An excellent book on Churchill . . . very readable way.** Peter Clarke. 2012. *Mr Churchill's Profession: Statesman, Orator, Writer*. London: Bloomsbury.

**page 158 ('about three times the earnings . . . at the time').** Geoffrey Wheatcroft. 'Winston Churchill, the author of victory'. 18 July 2012. *Times Literary Supplement*.

**page 164 Zoe Free . . . a real lifesaver'.** Peter Crush. 'The rise of the second job'. 20 April 2012. *Guardian*.

## CHAPTER 7: BEING YOUR OWN BOSS

**page 181 A study published in January 2013 . . . a more entrepreneurial environment'.** 'Female entrepreneurs could play crucial role in economic recovery but require greater support, new report finds'. 31 January 2013. Barclays Bank website. http://group.barclays.com/about-barclays/news/press-release-item/navigation-1329924296988?releaseID=2505.

**page 181 In the USA, as of 2012 . . . $1.3 trillion in revenue.** Susan Gregory Thomas. 'The rise of the female investor'. 22 February 2013. *Wall Street Journal.*

**page 181 Worldwide, thousands of women . . . stability over profit potential.** 'Why social enterprise attracts women'. 13 February 2013. *Green Futures Magazine* website. http://www.forumforthefuture.org/greenfutures/articles/why-social-enterprise-attracts-women.

**page 183 When it comes to entrepreneurship . . . more risk-aware than men.** See the GEM UK 2011 report on the Global Entrepreneurship Monitor website. http://www.gemconsortium.org/docs/2425/gem-uk-2011-report. Visited 17 January 2014.

**page 183 'If you have the power . . . and create new products.'** 'Why social enterprise attracts women'. *Green Futures Magazine.*

**page 192 According to a study of more than 20,000 businesses . . . in charge of the finances.** Kathryn Hopkins. 'Women more successful than men at getting bank loans'. 8 June 2013. *Times.*

**page 197 Women find equity investors hard . . . according to Erika Watson.** '6 ways in which accessing finance is different for women'. 6 September 2012. Startups website. http://startups.co.uk/6-ways-in-which-accessing- finance-is-different-for-women/.

**page 199 Kinopto, a cinema server solution . . . launch their product to market.** 'Case study: Kinopto'. Crowdcube website. http://www.crowdcube.com/pg/case-study-kinopto-76. Visited 17 January 2014.

**page 199 Gem Misa, founder . . . to fund future growth.** 'Case study: Righteous'. Crowdcube website. http://www.crowdcube.com/pg/case-study-righteous-57. Visited 17 January 2014.

**page 207 Women do better than men . . . thorough in their applications.** '6 ways in which accessing finance is different for women'. Startups.

## CHAPTER 8: THE SAVING HABIT

**page 215 Save £10 a month . . . and it will be £7,362.49.** 'Monthly or lump sum savings calculator'. This is Money website. http://www.thisismoney.co.uk/money/saving/article-1633419/Monthly-lump-sum-savings-calculator.html. Visited 19 January 2014.

**page 215 If you earn £25,000 a year . . . will be £1,651.55.** 'Take-home tax [sic] calculator'. http://www.thesalarycalculator.co.uk/salary.php. Visited 19 January 2014.

**page 216 You give your child £1 . . . four specific areas.** Michelle McGagh. 'How to show children the value of their pocket money'. 13 April 2012. Citywire Money ('The Lolly') website. http://citywire.co.uk/money/how-to-show-children-the-value-of-their-pocket-money/a581531.

**page 221 You can register your club . . . track your portfolio online.** See the ProShare Investment Clubs website. http://www.proshareclubs.co.uk/. Visited 3 February 2014.

**page 224 One in ten people say . . . lost their pension paperwork.** Simon Read. 'A quarter of adults have lost a pension pot, says survey'. 11 April 2013. *Independent*.

**page 224 If you think you may have lost track . . . Pension Tracing Service.** See https://www.gov.uk/find-lost-pension. Visited 3 February 2014.

**page 225 If you want to apply by post . . . Bank of England's website.** See http://www.bankofengland.co.uk/banknotes/pages/about/exchanges.aspx. Visited 3 February 2014.

**page 225 If they are really old banknotes . . . this may be the case.** See, for example, http://www.britishnotes.co.uk/news_and_info/valuemybanknotes/index.php. Visited 3 February 2014.

## CHAPTER 9: DOING GOOD

**page 241 Alicia Legg . . . donated to her former employer.** Fran R. Schumer. 'A curator, her garden and her art'. 10 June 1987. *New York Times*.

**page 242 The founder of 'Confessional Art' . . . $10.7 million.** 'Louise Bourgeois (1911–2010) Spider'. See the Christie's website. http://www.christies.com/lotfinder/sculptures-statues-figures/louise-bourgeois-spider-5496701-details.aspx. Visited 19 January 2014.

**page 243 Dame Vivien Duffield . . . children and young people.** 'Londoner of the day: Philanthropist Dame Vivien Duffield'. 24 March 2011. London24 website. http://www.london24.com/news/londoner_of_the_day_philanthropist_dame_vivien_duffield_1_840385.

**page 243 Arianna Huffington . . . in a speech to Smith College.** Arianna Huffington's Smith College commencement speech on 'Redefining success: The third metric'. 19 May 2013. *Huffington Post.*

**page 244 Research has identified eight mechanisms . . . charitable giving.** René Bekkers and Pamala Wiepking. 2011. 'A literature review of empirical studies of philanthropy: Eight mechanisms that drive charitable giving'. *Nonprofit and Voluntary Sector Quarterly* 40 (5), 924–73. The others are awareness of need, solicitation, costs and benefits, altruism, reputation and efficacy.

**page 244 A further study which examined two of these . . . taken into account).** Debra J. Mesch, Melissa S. Brown, Zachary I. Moore and Amir Daniel Hayat. 2011. 'Gender differences in charitable giving'. *International Journal of Nonprofit and Voluntary Sector Marketing*, 16 (4), 342–55.

**page 244 Sara Blakely, founder . . . $25 million in the bank.** Anya Kamenetz. 'Will women billionaires make better philanthropists?' 21 May 2013. *Co.Exist* online newsletter. http://www.fastcoexist.com/1682106/will-women-billionaires-make-better-philanthropists.

**page 245 In the UK, women occupy . . . 45 per cent of directors.** Ama Marston. 'Are not-for-profits getting away lightly on female leadership?' 9 July 2013. *Guardian.*

**page 245 I am passionate about employability . . . addresses social mobility in the process.** Entry is by open competition. See the Taylor Bennett Foundation website. http://www.taylorbennettfoundation.org/.

**page 246 Jane Shepherdson, CEO of Whistles . . . with my professional life.'** Sam Baker. 'Karma millionaires'. 26 May 2013. *Sunday Times.*

**page 247 BBC newsreader Mishal Husain . . . British Asian community.'** Ibid.

**page 248 In the USA, seven out of ten women . . . various charities annually.** 'Some facts about women entrepreneurs'. Go 4 Funding website. http://www.go4funding.com/Articles/Entrepreneur/Some-Facts-About-Women-Entrepreneurs.aspx. Visited 19 January 2014.

**page 248 Crowdfunding is an approach to raising capital . . . revenue sharing).** For more information visit the industry website. www.crowdsourcing.org. Visited 19 January 2014.

**page 249 Kickstarter, a crowdfunding platform . . . absolutely key.'** Judith Duffy. 'In with the in crowd'. 11 May 2013. *Herald Scotland.*

**page 250 Sisters Amy and Lucy Smith . . . for another entrepreneur.'** 'How recycling a loan can really make a difference'. 2 November 2011. *The Co-operative Magazine.* http://www.co-operative.coop/magazine/ethical-living/be-inspired/how-recycling-a-loan-can-make-a-difference/.

**page 250 New Philanthropy Capital . . . philanthropists are getting involved.** Abigail Rotheroe, Iona Joy, Plum Lomax and Sarah Hedley. 2013. *Best to Invest? A Funders' Guide to Social Investment.* London: NPC Publications. Available to download from http://www.thinknpc.org/publications/best-to-invest/.

**page 251 The Gift Aid Scheme increases the value . . . on the grossed-up value.** James Charles. 'Give to charity and take from the taxman'. 2 June 2013. *Sunday Times.*

**page 253 Sir Ian Wood CBE . . . your head must come into it too.'** 'Sir Ian Wood is a philanthropist who thinks, and acts, both locally and globally'. Philanthropy Impact website. http://www.philanthropy-impact.org/inspiration/personal-stories/sir-ian-wood. Visited 19 January 2014.

**page 254 'I definitely think leaving kids . . . in early 2013.** 'Bill Gates tells Reddit AMA: I won't leave kids "massive amount of money", will chair jump'. 11 February 2013. *Huffington Post.*

**page 255 'I would argue that when your kids . . . into the process.'** Carol J. Loomis. 'A conversation with Warren Buffett'. 25 June 2006. *Fortune.*

**page 255 By 2013, the charity had raised . . . twenty-five years.** See the Will Aid website. http://www.willaid.org.uk/. Visited 3 February 2014.

**page 255 Currently, only 7 per cent . . . boost legacy income.** James Charles. 'Give to charity'.

**page 256 A study by the government's . . . it will be bigger.** Owain Service and Michael Sanders. 12 July 2013. 'Behavioural insights and charitable giving'. Civil Service Quarterly blog. https://quarterly.blog.gov.uk/2013/07/12/behavioural-insights-and-charitable-giving/.

**page 257 The responsible consumer is someone who . . . natural world.** Jacqueline Payne. 'Ethical consumerism and conservatism – hand in glove'. 26 January

2012. *The Heinz Journal* online publication by graduates of the Carnegie Mellon University. http://journal.heinz.cmu.edu/2012/01/ethical-consumerism-and-conservatism-hand-in-glove-2/.

**page 258 Research from Net Impact's . . . this is the case.** 'Talent report: What workers want in 2012'. Study by Net Impact and Rutgers University. Available to download from https://netimpact.org/learning-resources/research/what-workers-want. Visited 20 January 2014.

**page 258 And a GreenBiz analysis in 2013 . . . ethical and social commitments.** Ellen Weinreb. 'At work, do women care more than men about sustainability?'. 20 February 2013. GreenBiz website. http://www.greenbiz.com/blog/2013/02/20/work-do-women-care-more-men-about-sustainability.

**page 258 In their book *Making Good* . . . which is good for business.** Dev Aujla and Billy Parish. 2012. *Making Good: Finding Meaning, Money and Community in a Changing World*. New York, NY: Rodale Books.

## CHAPTER 10: BEING PREPARED FOR WHEN THINGS DON'T GO TO PLAN

**page 275 An article in the *Sunday Times* featured . . . how much they can claim in a settlement.** Catherine Wheatley. 'We stick together for the company: Couples whose marriages break up don't have to stop running their firms'. 14 April 2013. *Sunday Times*.

# USEFUL RESOURCES

## CHAPTER 1: YOUR FINANCIAL GOALS (or MONEY IS NOT BORING)

page 22 www.thesalarycalculator.co.uk: calculate how much you earn on a weekly/daily/hourly basis.

page 29 www.which.co.uk: reviews products and services, so that you make the best purchase decisions for your needs.

page 29 www.moneysavingexpert.com: consumer website dedicated to cutting your bills.

page 30 www.moneysupermarket.com: price comparison website.

page 30 www.gocompare.com: price comparison website.

## CHAPTER 2: CUTTING THE COST OF EVERYDAY LIFE

page 38 www.myvouchercodes.co.uk: provides voucher codes, discount codes and discount vouchers updated daily for the UK's leading online stores.

page 45 www.seat61.com: offers deals and help with booking trains across borders.

page 49 www.moneysupermarket.com/credit-cards: compare hundreds of credit cards instantly.

page 51 www.mobilife.com: mobile phone price comparison site.

page 51 www.billmonitor.com: mobile phone price comparison site.

page 51 www.wandera.com: provides businesses with control and visibility of their mobile data usage.

page 51 www.snappli.com: compresses, optimizes and secures mobile internet data usage.

page 51 www.techradar.com: consumer technology news and review site.

page 52 www.imeasure.org.uk: monitors your home or organization's weekly energy consumption.

page 52 www.uswitch.com: compares prices for a range of energy, personal finance, insurance and communications services.

page 54 www.ayearwithoutsupermarkets.com: one couple's commitment to buy food only from local, small shops and markets.

page 54 www.couponmom.com: US website providing coupons for all fifty states.

page 55 www.agirlcalledjack.com: Jack Monroe's blog offering delicious budget recipes.

page 56 www.mystery-shoppers.co.uk: specialists in mystery shopping and customer satisfaction research, including how to apply to become a mystery shopper.

page 57 www.streetlife.com: local social network with the aim of helping people make the most of where they live by connecting and sharing with neighbours.

page 57 www.blablacar.com: connects drivers with empty seats to passengers looking for a ride.

page 57 www.zipcar.co.uk: car sharing company providing automobile reservations to its members, billable by the hour or day.

page 59 www.mumsnet.com: tips on cost savings for families, plus forums where users share peer-to-peer advice and information on parenting, products and many other issues.

page 62 www.justfortheloveofit.org (now part of www.streetbank.com): puts you in touch with your community so you can lend and borrow your neighbours' everyday objects and skills.

page 62 www.ecomodo.com: lend and borrow each other's everyday objects, skills and spaces.

page 62 www.homelink.org.uk: house exchange organization.

## CHAPTER 3: PROPERTY (or HOW TO SPEND A LOT OF MONEY)

page 75 www.bbc.co.uk/homes/property/mortgagecalculator.shtml: calculate your monthly mortgage payments.

page 89 www.helptobuy.org.uk: government scheme helping those who are looking to buy a property for up to £600,000.

page 91 www.ukauctionlist.com: buy or sell property at auction in the UK.

page 91 www.primelocation.com/guides/buying/how-to-buy-a-property-at-auction/: helpful article by Lucy Alexander giving advice about buying a property at auction.

page 101 www.deedoftrust.co.uk: provides expertly drafted deeds helping protect your interests in property.

CHAPTER 4: DEALING WITH DEBT

page 110 www.payplan.com: offers debt management plans and free debt advice.

page 132 www.citizensadvice.org.uk: provides free legal and money advice.

page 132 www.nationaldebtline.co.uk: helpline providing free debt advice.

page 132 www.stepchange.org: consumer credit counselling service providing free debt advice.

page 133 www.debtadvicefoundation.org: provides free debt advice.

page 133 www.capuk.org: national charity working to lift people out of debt and poverty.

page 134 www.bis.gov.uk/insolvency: insolvency service website.

page 134 www2.crw.gov.uk/pr/: consumer credit register.

page 138 www.experian.co.uk: check your credit rating.

page 138 www.equifax.co.uk: check your credit rating.

CHAPTER 5: GETTING FINANCIALLY LITERATE

page 149 www.financetalking.com: specialists in financial training for non-financial people, corporate communications, financial PR and investor relations.

page 153 www.academictrader.org: online economics and business courses from faculty at the world's top universities.

page 153 www.alison.com: leading provider of free online courses with certificates for basic and essential workplace skills (tailored to the USA).

page 153 www.cimaglobal.com: find out more about the Chartered Institute of Management Accountants qualification.

page 154 www2.accaglobal.com/uk: global body for professional accountants, offering the Chartered Certified Accountant qualification.

page 154 www.cfainstitute.org: a global association of investment professionals offering a number of programmes including the Chartered Financial Analyst (CFA) designation.

## CHAPTER 6: EARNING MORE

page 160 www.linkedin.com: social networking website for people in professional occupations.

page 165 www.peopleperhour.com: find and hire skilled freelancers.

page 168 www.findaparty.co.uk: find a home party plan consultant to hold a product party in your own home.

page 171 www.crashpadder.com (now part of Airbnb): pay to advertise your room.

page 171 www.mondaytofriday.com: advertise and find homes, desks and meeting places for the working week.

page 171 www.spareroom.co.uk: advertise a room in your house or flat for free.

**page 172** www.airbnb.co.uk: community marketplace for people to list and rent accommodation around the world for a shorter period of time.

**page 172** www.holidaylettings.co.uk: advertises privately owned holiday cottages, villas and apartments worldwide.

**page 172** www.film-locations.co.uk: register your home for free on leading London and UK film, TV and photo location agency.

**page 172** www.locationworks.com: location agency supplying locations for filming, photography, television, drama, commercials and events.

**page 172** www.shootfactory.co.uk: film, TV and photo location agency.

**page 173** www.yourparkingspace.co.uk: find parking spaces and garages to rent, or profit through renting out your off-street car parking space, driveway or garage.

**page 173** www.parkatmyhouse.com: find cheap car parking, or rent out your parking space, garage or driveway.

**page 173** www.getaround.com: online car sharing service that allows drivers to rent cars from private car owners, and owners to rent out their cars for payment.

**page 173** www.storemates.co.uk: find storage space in your community and earn money through renting out your extra space.

**page 173** www.spareground.co.uk: rent out your property, driveway, garage, shed, attic, garden, paddock, allotment or other land you may own.

**page 173** www.storenextdoor.com: rent out your spare storage space or find storage space in your area.

**page 174** www.rentmyitems.com: rent out your tools, sports equipment, furniture or skills.

## CHAPTER 7: BEING YOUR OWN BOSS

**page 186** www.startupdonut.co.uk/startup/business-planning/writing-a-business-plan: guide to starting a new business, offering free resources, advice and tools.

**page 186** www.princes-trust.org.uk/need-help/enterprise-programme/explore-where-to-start/business-plans/business-plan-templates.aspx: offers a business plan guide and templates.

**page 195** www.gov.uk/understanding-the-enterprise-finance-guarantee: understanding the Enterprise Finance Guarantee (EFG) scheme.

**page 196** www.startuploans.co.uk: government-funded scheme to provide loans and mentors for entrepreneurs.

**page 196** www.prowess.org.uk/facts: women's enterprise and entrepreneurship facts and statistics.

**page 196** www.fundingcircle.com: provides loans to small businesses, funded by thousands of individual investors.

**page 196** www.zopa.com: peer-to-peer lending.

**page 196** www.socialbaank.com: not-for-profit organization helping people get into business by lending up to £1,000 to new borrowers.

**page 197** www.cdfa.org.uk: provides support to people setting up community finance organizations.

page 198 www.crowdcube.com: equity crowdfunding platform for starting up and growing businesses.

page 198 www.seedrs.com: crowdfunding equity website for seed-stage companies.

page 205 www.marketinvoice.com: online invoice auction service.

page 210 www.gov.uk/write-business-plan: download free business plan templates and find help and advice on how to write your business plan.

page 210 www.bawe-uk.org: British Association of Women Entrepreneurs, a peer group for women entrepreneurs who want to be challenged.

page 210 www.elmline.co.uk: award-winning social enterprise providing low-cost loans.

page 210 www.fcem.org/home.php?lang=en: association for like-minded women who share an interest in entrepreneurship.

page 210 www.isbe.org.uk/facts: facts and figures about women's enterprise from the Institute for Small Business and Entrepreneurship.

page 210 www.thehappystartupschool.com: help with setting up a business.

page 210 www.wibn.co.uk: Women in Business Network operating monthly meetings.

## CHAPTER 8: THE SAVING HABIT

page 219 www.fundsmith.co.uk: a low-cost global equity fund with ISA and Junior ISA options, available to direct investors.

page 222 www.stocktrade.co.uk: group of independently owned private client investment managers offering an online ISA service.

page 223 www.gov.uk/child-trust-funds/overview: find out where your child's CTF is held.

page 223 www.mylostaccount.org.uk: trace your lost accounts and savings.

page 224 www.nsandi.com/savings-premium-bonds-have-i-won: find out if you have an unclaimed Premium Bond prize.

page 225 www.gov.uk/find-lost-pension: use the UK government's Pension Tracing Service, to find a lost pension.

page 225 www.bankofengland.co.uk: exchange banknotes that have been withdrawn from circulation.

page 225 www.thecurrencycommission.com: continue exchanging old outstanding banknotes into euros, US or Canadian dollars.

page 235 www.proshareclubs.co.uk: provides information on starting up and running an investment club.

## CHAPTER 9: DOING GOOD

page 246 www.thinknpc.org: helps charities and funders to work more effectively.

page 247 www.speakers4schools.org: charity providing state schools with talks from inspiring leaders of industry, for free.

page 249 www.kickstarter.com: crowdfunding platform.

page 250 www.lendwithcare.org: microfinance lending initiative.

page 251 www.hmrc.gov.uk/individuals/giving/payroll.htm: giving to charity through your payslip or pension.

page 251 www.cafonline.org: charity which aims to improve the way donations are made and how charities handle their finance.

page 253 www.philanthropy-impact.org: making sense of and inspiring philanthropy across borders, sectors and causes.

page 253 www.sharegift.org: charity which provides a solution to the business problem of small shareholdings by converting them into cash for charities.

page 255 www.willaid.org.uk: find a local solicitor to write your will in exchange for a donation to charity.

page 261 www.ethicalconsumer.org: ethical consumer magazine.

page 261 www.goodgym.org: get fit by doing good.

page 261 www.instituteforphilanthropy.org: helping donors achieve impact.

## CHAPTER 10: BEING PREPARED FOR WHEN THINGS DON'T GO TO PLAN

page 272 www.protectyourbubble.com: insurance for your gadgets.

page 276 www.adviceuk.org.uk: the UK's largest support network for free, independent advice centres.